The God Gap

by

George Nelson Thompson

A GUIDE

FOR

PRAYER

BOOK 1

Copyright © 1980 by George Nelson Thompson
P. O. Box 1811, Thousand Oaks, CA 91360

ISBN 0-940564-02-5

Bible quotations from the Revised Standard Version of the Bible, copyrighted 1946, 1952, © 1971, 1973.

THE CHALLENGE

Many Christians wish they practiced regularly a daily pattern of Bible reading and prayer. They honestly admit they do not, although from time to time in the past they have tried to begin.

The organized Christian Church, or, more properly, Christian Church leaders, have not been very helpful, in practical ways, to assist the earnest Christian to overcome the difficulties involved. One can go farther. Christian leaders have failed to teach their people. In the light of the Church's teaching, this failure strains credence unless it is assigned to doubt about the very existence of God.

A. J. Ayer and his fellow logical positivists tell us that God is meaningless. The influence of this kind of use of language has invaded every thought pattern of the modern world.

We hear a lot about "gaps," the Generation Gap, the Missile Gap, the Credibility Gap and some others. One that is the most significant in our times is getting the least attention, *The God Gap.*

A frustrating aspect of our times is the obvious inability today to recognize evil, perversity, and sin. Our acceptance of the most bizarre depravity, the reversal of all norms, shows one of the most dangerous trends a society can take, loss of ability to establish values.

What is right? What is moral? What is godly?

Does anyone seriously believe that God is an objective reality, the One with whom we may have personal dealings, and not just a subjective wish thought that what one hopes is true is really true?

The problem of prayer, I contend, is not just the crucial issue of religion for our time, but the only problem religiously which has current validity for exclusive attention.

This book assumes the objective reality of the existence of a caring God.

There is here an attempt to provide step-by-step practical help in what has always been regarded as minimal and essential for living of the Christian life, the daily use of the Bible for faith and practice and daily prayer for each Christian to seek God's guidance. Why?

To transform believers and the world to the ways of God by the pervasive sweetening of life.

George Nelson Thompson

PSALM 78

Give ear, O my people, to my
  teaching;
    incline your ears to the words of
    my mouth!
2 I will open my mouth in a parable;
    I will utter dark sayings from of old,
3 things that we have heard and known,
    that our fathers have told us.
4 We will not hide them from their children,
    but tell to the coming generation
  the glorious deeds of the LORD, and his
  might,
    and the wonders which he has
    wrought.

TABLE OF CONTENTS

FOREWORD

Every Christian would agree that prayer is important. Clergy urge their people to pray. Many books have been written about prayer. Yet few people feel comfortable praying. They just do not know how.

The one weakness evident in this area of Christian concern, in any church, is the absence of practical and clear step-by-step procedures which must be followed to learn how to pray.

"Teach us how to pray," Jesus' disciples asked.

No less is asked or needed by Christians today.

Prayer Does Things

George A. Buttrick, in 1942, in *Prayer* summed up some of the values of prayer. Prayer is a challenge to man and his world, a detractor of man's logical systems. Prayer still is the doorway to mystery and the supernatural. Prayer is the answer to crises, problems and difficult decisions.

Let us assume that the pleadings of the clergy to pray are being heard, and that the books available on prayer are being read. Apparently none of these efforts are getting through to people.

A number of years ago, a national weekly magazine contained an article purporting to answer the question, "What sermons do people want to hear today?" A cross section of the population had been polled. The number one choice was *How Can I Make Prayer More Effective.*

Would this be your choice?

How Willing Are You?

The plea today seems to be the ancient one, "Teach us to pray (Lk.11:1)."

Our age has an aversion to spiritual struggle. We seek easy answers to difficult questions. How willing are you — and it must be personalized, *you* — how willing are *you* to delve deeply into the problems of prayer?

How determined are you?

If you are both willing and determined, the chapters which follow will lead you gradually into deeper and deeper thought, and you will be taught how to pray.

To Begin

The following initial suggestions are offered about how to use this book, many of which will be repeated later in different contexts. *They must be repeated. You must understand at this stage their importance.* There are four suggestions:

- choose a time and place for your reading which will remain the same daily. Plan for a range of 15-30 minutes. Do not exceed this time. Later you may wish to do more.

- let it be a place where you can be relaxed and be able to take notes, preparing yourself with a Bible, a dictionary, and writing material. Any translation of the Bible you prefer is suitable, although you may wish to have a cheaper edition so you are able to mark passages and write in the margins.

- read this book slowly for understanding: read, stop, think, write (if you have anything to note) — read, stop, etc.

- do not jump ahead in your reading.

When you are out of shape physically, you do not lunge into hours of exercise the first week, unless you are foolish. You exercise moderately, gradually. The same principle applies in learning how to pray.

How many people do you know — perhaps you — with determination to "be good" or turn "spiritual" overnight, vigorously launch a program to read the Bible from cover to cover, a chapter a day, beginning with Genesis?

When did they — you — quit, the second or third day? Or, did they last one or two weeks?

SUGGESTION

Be appalled, O heavens, at this,
    be shocked, be utterly desolate,
        says the Lord,
for my people have committed two
      evils:
    they have forsaken me,
the fountain of living waters,
    and hewed out cisterns for
      themselves,
broken cisterns,
    that can hold no water.

— Jeremiah 2:12-13

In an exploratory way, turn to the passage given above in the Old Testament book of Jeremiah, Chapter 2, verses 12 and 13.

Read a few passages before these and a few after these.
Determine the context. Use your dictionary if you need help.
Turn all the words over in your mind, slowly, then full sentences.
Reread them. Reflect on them.

Nothing predetermined is supposed to happen, but something might happen: a new idea or insight, questions. Write it down, even if silly.

GUIDE FOR ALL HOLY SCRIPTURES (memorize):

Hear them, read, mark, learn, and inwardly digest them.

Why do I ask you to do this? Martin Luther writes:

If you want to obtain grace, then see to it that you hear the Word of God attentively or meditate on it diligently. The Word, I say, and only the Word, is the vehicle of God's grace.

EZEKIEL 36

26 A new heart I will give you, and a new spirit I will put within you; and I will take out of your flesh the heart of stone and give you a heart of flesh. 27 And I will put my spirit within you, and cause you to walk in my statutes and be careful to observe my ordinances. 28 You shall dwell in the land which I gave to your fathers; and you shall be my people, and I will be your God.

INTRODUCTION TO PRAYER

Purpose and Approach

The purpose of these books is to aim to teach Christians both the importance of and possibility for a genuinely significant personal prayer life. The approach of this book is threefold:

--- specific instruction and motivation to develop a pattern of disciplined prayer by using regularly the Holy Scriptures.

--- a daily reading for the initial and crucial first three months of effort.

--- an educationally/theologically/Biblically-oriented questioning process throughout to aid each reader to develop his own patterns of prayer.

Many Ways to Learn

The reference to three approaches, or elements, to prayer is not meant to imply that there are *only* three ways to teach people how to pray. It is suggested, however, that these three elements *in combination* are neglected ones in the personal prayer lives of the majority of Christians.

Prayer is learned, as will amply be made clear in the pages ahead, by endless combinations of intertwining and consciously adopted new habits.

The effort here is simply to call attention to or emphasize three elements which ought to be substituted for the all-too-common practices of badgering and scolding used to coerce and shame people to pray.

Above all, of course, God through the Holy Spirit — in His ineffable and mysterious ways — teaches us all to pray according to what is best and necessary for each one of us.

Christian but Non-Denominational

This book is directed, therefore, toward answering the questions and problems of those who seriously want to learn to pray.

Non-denominational in content, this book nevertheless attempts to make use of the best of the heritage of the whole Christian Church of the past about prayer. At the same time, there is a redirecting of people's minds within the scope of modern life and its problems to thinking relevantly once again about prayer as a present option and reality.

A Personal Discovery

I first learned how to pray (having thought I knew) after having been in the active ministry of the Christian Church for more than ten years, when the necessity for divine aid was forced upon me by a series of personal crises. In 1950 my wife was dying, the result of a crippling stroke brought on by the closing of her heart's mitral valve. My professional life, in addition, was at low ebb.

Literally, I was driven into a life situation too much for me to handle. My years of theological education, having been the pastor of two successful churches, and several years as a teacher in philosophy and religion had not provided the answers I needed for the way out. Through learning how to pray, for the first time, I was given what I lacked, a power from God to sustain and direct me.

Academic Answers

Many years later, when my wife had recovered from her illness through a first heart surgery and the personal and professional crises had been resolved, I regarded what I had learned about the power of prayer — God's power — as purely personal and subjective experiences.

If I talked about prayer and this period of my life to others, I was extremely careful to couch my language in academic and non-personal terminology.

Why the Reluctance?

The significance of my attitude and approach should be underscored. Did I believe, then, that I had helped myself?

No. My own resources had collapsed completely. Powerless myself, I had experienced sustaining power outside myself to do what I thought I could not do, and knew I could not do alone, resolve the problems and go on.

The full explanation for my reluctance to speak freely and naturally to others about what I had learned about God through prayer I do not, even these many years later, readily discern. If I was afraid of what others might say about me if I spoke openly about believing in God's direct involvement in my life, I was not truly aware of this fear.

I believe one explanation for the cautious handling of my discoveries — for I 'discovered' something daily — was unwillingness to deal glibly with what had deeply touched me to the core. I also discovered that there were many traps into which one could fall in the continuing development of one's spiritual life by boasting of progress made.

Involved also was the fact that for a long time I thought what I had come to know during extreme crisis was commonly known to many Christians — *according to their words, at any rate.* Therefore, I felt my prayer experiences were nothing remarkable in themselves except to me.

Growing Awareness

Fortunately, growth is characteristic of those who have been forced into the knowledge of the combination of one's own inadequacies and how God works through them.

I did not remain in the frame of mind where I talked about prayer only in academic language. Furthermore, it began to dawn on me that perhaps the words of others about prayer in fact might come from ignorance or be used to hide what was really not known to them.

To be very candid (I include myself here), this is a particularly easy deception for those who are skilled, as clergy are, in formulating language for public reception.

This growing awareness led me one day suddenly to realize that by my silence I was doing to those I pastored and taught what had probably been done to me by my own pastors, teachers, and friends. *They, when they had come to know prayer's amazing values and powers — if they really knew — had also regarded the subject as too personal and too intimate to discuss freely and openly with others.* Of course, I recognized as well that it was entirely possible that the silence of some of these persons about the place of prayer in personal religion may have had its origin in the fact *that they knew nothing at all about prayer!*

A New Resolution

Once I became aware of my own shortcomings in this area, holding back and not explaining, it was then that I resolved to do everything in my power to teach people how to pray, especially dealing with the problems of prayer and answers to problems. The values of prayer are too obvious for me to restate them here, but what is not obvious is the confusion which surrounds the whole undertaking . . . *some can pray, and some cannot . . . you must have a flair for it . . . I just cannot get started . . . I am good for the first few days and, then . . . finished.*

There are problems. Honesty here is mandatory. That which is precious is always bought with a price. My wife, Luella, had three additional heart surgeries — in 1968, 1970, and 1972. God's sustaining power has never left either of us.

On the basis of the above, therefore, I can state factually that this book had its beginnings more than twenty-five years ago. Further, that what is presented here is the distilled version of many years of experimentation personally and in efforts through sermons and counseling of others to write simply, yet meaningfully, about Biblically-oriented meditative prayer.

The Special Problem

A special problem is present for our generation about prayer, the result of increasing scientific and technological developments in the 20th century. Early in the present century there were signs of an impending revolution among philosophers known as logical positivism *Philosophy was considered to be a*

7

reflection upon the sciences. If the function of philosophy, therefore, is to clarify the fundamentals and the structure of scientific knowledge, philosophy should have nothing to do with questions that are supposed to transcend such knowledge. The business of philosophers is to make it clear that questions incapable of empirical verification are profitless to pursue, since they are essentially meaningless.

Philosophy lost its independent and creative capacity, becoming not a reflection *upon* the sciences, but a reflection *of* the sciences. The positivists side-stepped conveniently the fact of knowledge being a philosophical issue and once-for-all closed the door to philosophy's considering any issues but the narrowest of arbitrary conclusions previously decided before examination of the most puzzling and long-standing philosophical questions men and women have been asking for thousands of years.

Still Appealing and Influential

Popularizing this narrow concept of philosophy was an Englishman, Alfred Julius Ayer, in his book *Language, Truth and Logic,* published in 1936.

"God is meaningless," wrote Ayer. Statements about the existence of God and similar religious utterances cannot evoke a philosopher's agnosticism, Ayer expanded, any more than they can elicit his belief or disbelief. For, since such statements are meaningless, they cannot properly be considered at all.

Ayer concluded that, " . . . there is no possibility of demonstrating the existence of a God. What is not so generally recognized is that there can be no way of proving that the existence of a God, such as the God of Christianity, is even probable."

Men and women of the 20th century found this view appealing and influential in light of the continuing revelations of science. Somehow, the mysteries revealed constantly as new information opened some doors were ignored as men and women came to believe they were giants on the earth.

Some Reactions

Arthur David Ritchie, a well-known Scottish philosopher, objected strenuously to logical positivism. He wrote, " . . . this theory I am sure is false and the mother of a great family of fallacies. It is plausible because it appeals to what we imagine to be immediate, certain, and actual, and because we do not realize that the sense data it has to drag in are purely mythical."

Coming closer to the religious issues facing us here is the view of George F. Thomas, an American philosopher:

If we try to avoid the problem of denying the possibility of a world view and contenting ourselves with the description of relations between natural phenomena, *as in Positivism,* we refuse to heed the highest demand of reason and to meet the deepest need of life itself.

Does God Exist?

Logical positivism has its roots in an ancient fallacy: that theological statements are meaningless if they do not originate in experience.

Christians today must follow the advice of St. Augustine: ". . . to expose the folly of that scepticism which argues solely on the ground of its own experiences, and has no faith in anything beyond."

Answer to the Problem

In the light of the Christian Church's teaching about God, His Will, His teachings, and His Holy Scriptures, the failure of church leaders to teach their people how to pray strains credence unless it is assigned to doubt about the very existence of God.

Have the logical positivists convinced Christians that to talk about God is meaningless?

The problem of prayer, I contend, is not just the crucial issue of religion for our time but the *only* problem religiously which has current validity for exclusive attention.

One must go directly to the heart of the problem, the objective reality of the existence of God who either can and does have dealings with men and women *or* cannot and does not have dealings with men and women. God is or *he*, the little one we call god, is not.

None can question the existence of the Church and its institutions, its members, its Holy Book, and a host of other obvious and very material and observable phenomena. *The objective reality of the existence of a caring God is the issue.*

Prayer squarely and exclusively hits at the core of this issue. Can one *know* God or only a subjective self?

What is wrong with the word *crucial,* rather than *only* as stated above? Does not *crucial* imply *decisive?*

The difficulty with the word *crucial,* as used prior to World War II, is that what was crucial then depended upon what was in vogue among Christian leaders. One week it might be that *social issues were crucial,* another week *political involvement was crucial,* and still a later time, *knowledge of the sources of the Pentateuch for interpretation of the whole of Biblical thought was crucial.*

Had prayer been regarded by Christians many decades ago as *crucial,* in its root sense, the gravity of the immediate problems facing the Christian Church today would not be so severe.

An Underground Church?

Society appears to be at a dead end precisely because individuals have reached the end of will power (there is no will but man's), which is too weak to be willed any longer, and all human resources normally used to answer the issues of our day have simply petered out.

That is why the issue of *prayer alone* is the central core out of which the fight is joined in and for our generation.

If the struggle of the existence of God is not faced, once again in our day, there may well come a time when Christianity will be forced to go underground and the Christian Church as we know it today will disappear from the face of the earth.

Perhaps this already is occurring.

Who Are the Christians?

Certainly, it may readily be admitted, Christians have no common agreement about the purpose of the Church today. The problem goes farther. Division and hatred characterize the people of many denominations today, within and without. Sides taken are likely to follow the pattern of the Crusades — mistaken causes for mistaken ends — leading to futility and death. The Church often responds irrationally to issues, being fully captive not to the law of Christ but to the mores of the cultural and political climate of our secular society.

What is the Church? Who can tell?

A political party, choosing sides? A social welfare group, having nothing but money or goods to give? A lobby, representing special interests? A show crowd, dispensing entertainment?

In the church today, the deed has now become the parent to the thought and works precede faith, the ancient heresy of Pelagianism come to life. A pelagian is one who is a follower of Pelagius (360?-420?), a British monk and theologian, denying original sin and holding that man has perfect freedom of the will.

The Only Hope

A genuine discovery of prayer — so God can be known — is the only hope of the Church today. Prayer is the *only* serious approach to the Church's and the world's problems members of the Christian Church have not tried.

Many Christians today lack genuineness in speaking to the needs of men and women of the twentieth century. The reason for this is that some of the clergy and laity alike have severed themselves from one essential reality, the living spring of Christian faith, personal and immediate knowledge and experience of the living God.

It is extremely dubious that Christians can find God only in the milling streets of current secular events and movements where, in the jargon of this school of thought, "God's reconciliation is breaking in." Finding God is primarily dependent upon the rediscovery of the Biblical "nowness" of God's breaking in on the individual soul; then only will personal life and any secular events and movements have genuine meaning.

The Sweetening of Life

Believers in the whole Church of Christ today should exert their influence toward what William Temple (1881-1944), Archbishop of Canterbury, called the pervasive sweetening of life and of all human relationships:

... there is the pervasive sweetening of life and of all human relationships, by those who carry with them something of the mind of Christ, received from Christian upbringing, from prayer and meditation, and from communion. No particular enterprise, nor all of them together, can compare with the influence so exerted. To this extent they are justified who say that the task of the Church in face of social problems is to make good Christian men and women. That is by far its most important contribution.

Under existing social and cultural conditions and under the conditions facing Christians in Christian congregations today, it is not easy for anyone to be a man or a woman of prayer. The one constant gap facing any of us is separatedness from God.

Closing the God-gap through prayer must begin first with *you*.

Adults who are unwilling to reeducate themselves periodically are doomed to mediocrity.

—James A. Michener

Chapter 1

THE CLUTTERED ROAD

Earlier I stated that I believed this book was unique in its approach to prayer. It is the purpose of this chapter to examine some of the other approaches to prayer which claim attention. The road is cluttered with many possibilities.

Denominational Guides

There are many denominational daily devotional guides. All of them direct the reader to the Bible. Still, ignorance about the Bible is at an all-time high. The Bible is still a best seller. Yet few Christians even attempt to read the Bible, or to examine carefully and follow its precepts.

Have these other devotional guides failed to do what they were designed to do? It is difficult if not impossible to determine. Since they are printed year after year, they must fill some kind of need.

Obviously, though, they are not read by the great majority of Christians. The existing daily devotional guides suffer the same fate as Bible reading. In fact, there might be some justification to blame these guides for Biblical ignorance. The assumption seems to be that if these are read, the necessary Biblical information will somehow come through to the believer.

There are signs that these guides have failed in their purpose. One cannot say human nature is weak and lacks will power, attributing to this the cause for lack of reading either the Bible or the daily devotional guides.

The writing and approach of the great majority of the existing daily devotional guides in the main are evasive of genuine issues, patronizing the thinking Christian, filled with platitudes, sentimentalities, or self-centered.

Polite Messages

Modern books about daily Bible reading and daily personal devotions may fail simply because of their poor theology or because they are not written in the style of the Holy Scriptures. Or, they give a passing nod to the Scriptures and emphasize the positive power of self alone.

Why should not modern Christian books avail themselves of the Bible as a model? The style of the Bible is blunt, direct, challenging, disturbing, relevant to human conditions, and forceful with the power of God.

Most devotional guides consist of polite messages which strike one as quiet talks down sentimental pathways, poor attempts to "explain" the plain words of Scripture, and encourage the reader to be satisfied with Christian platitudes he has heard all his life.

Would that such devotional guides were either cold or hot! Because they are lukewarm, they should suffer the same fate as the works of the church in Laodicea and be spewed out of the mouth (Rev. 3:15-16).

What About the Classics?

The known classics of devotional literature have a double weakness. One, as is true for "classics" in other fields of literature, they are frequently talked about, but seldom read.

Second, the classics are largely captive to pre-Reformation monastic asceticism in their frame of reference. They do not touch genuinely either the needs or the lifestyles of modern men and women.

Each age needs a new approach to prayer, as does our generation. However, this does not mean a rejection of lessons learned in the past.

A Neglected Approach

For example, the approach to prayer of Martin Luther (1483-1546), the German reformer, is completely neglected and unknown today even among many Lutherans.

Luther uniquely found his way into the presence of God and knew, by his own personal experience, that the living God was accessible to every Christian.

The Bible as the Word of God, to Luther, was the path to God. Luther taught men and women to read the Bible in a new way. His teachings are extraordinarily helpful to speak to men and women of the 20th Century about prayer and the reading of God's Word.

The Directness of Scripture

If read properly, the Bible will comfort, please, uplift, but often the reader will be shocked. The Bible, as it were, gets under the reader's skin, frustrates his mind with assumptions he is not ready to accept, and bruises his sensibilities.

In other words, like the Cross, the Gospel Message (Old and New Testaments) is "a stumbling block to Jews and folly to Gentiles (I Cor. 1:23)."

Jesus castigates the scribes and Pharisees. He calls the Pharisees hypocrites (Mt. 22:18) and preaches "woe" against the scribes and Pharisees (Mt. 23:13-36). They are called by Jesus blind fools, blind guides, full of extortion and rapacity, whitewashed tombs full of dead men's bones and all uncleanness, full of iniquity, and murderers.

Paul opposed Peter because Peter acted insincerely and was not straightforward (Gal. 2:11-21).

Why is this language and approach so characteristic of the Bible? One, there is a great Gospel to be preached for all men, one so important to require direct and plain speech.

Two, the followers of Jesus Christ were fully acquainted with the world in which they lived, as were the Old Testament prophets as well, knowing all the challenges of the secular world and how resistant the world and its people were to change.

Three, plain speech gets results. One may not agree with such language, but there can be no doubt about what was said. It worked for the 1st Century Christians. Why should it not work in the 20th Century?

All of the above three characteristics, I contend, should be the style and language of a modern approach to Bible reading and prayer. The aim? *The truth.* The rest will follow.

One cannot hope to achieve the perfect success of the Bible in this regard, but I think a Christian writer should be faulted if he does not try.

The public relations approach to Christianity, in vogue in the United States for half a century, is a sham.

Men and women are dying. The country is losing its soul. Churches are faltering. Dissillusionment with morality and law is commonplace. Violence seems, for many, to be the only direct and honest way out of injustices. None can trust his neighbor.

Transcendental Meditation

The Christian Church today has lost influence. A vacuum has been created in the lives of many people. The mind and spirit abhor a vacuum. One of the eastern religions which has taken the place once occupied by Christian thought is known as Transcendental Meditation (TM).

TM purports to solve problems and to aid the meditator to reach many goals in personal living, in business affairs, and in personal relations. Can TM accomplish the same results as Christian meditative-prayer?

According to its proponents, TM may become for you, without the use of drugs and depending upon your personal needs, either a downer or an upper, calm you or heighten your awareness. All you need to do as a TMer, after you have paid your substantial fee, is to sit still for 20 minutes each morning and evening and silently repeat, over and over again, a specially designed (for you personally) secret Sanskrit word, or *mantra.* This exercise is a cure-all, thousands of sincere chanters believe, for everything from high blood pressure to poor relationships with others.

Flight from Reality?

According to some of its literature, TM makes no claim to be either a religion or a philosophy, a view hotly contested by some who point out that TM is a form of Hinduism and involves the meditator in a specific eastern religious philosophy of life. A dangerous exercise, say others, leading to "flight from reality" and "premature entry into higher states of consciousness."

Meditation/Transcendental?

In *How To Meditate,* Lawrence LeShan, a practicing psychotherapist as well as a meditator (not TM), puts this form of meditation into a balanced perspective. TM is but one division within one of ten or more major forms of meditation commonly practiced by eastern religious practitioners: Breath Counting, the Bubble, the Thousand-Petaled Lotus, the Safe Harbor, and others.

The twin goals of all these many forms of meditation and the mystical path, writes LeShan, are:

> ... the attainment of a second way of com-
> prehending reality and the increased seren-
> ity and competence in being.

Based upon this statement and normal dictionary definitions, TM, it appears to me, is improperly named. TM is neither *transcendental* nor *meditation.*

Transcendental: a philosophy that asserts the primacy of the spiritual and transcendental over the material and empirical.

Meditation: to engage in contemplation or reflection; contemplate: to view or consider with continued attention; reflect: think, conceive, cogitate, reason, and deliberate.

TM may be more a bodily-relaxing program than a thinking-reflecting, engaging   in reasoning form of meditation. The same results can be obtained from certain forms of physical exercise or by Breath Counting.

TM parts company from all thinkers and true meditation: Plato to Whitehead and Augustine to Tillich.

The Telephone Book Method of Meditation

LeShan believes nonsense phrases have a value for the relaxing-meditation form. His favorite method of designing a *mantra* he calls LeShan's Telephone Book Method, which he believes as effective as any other. LeShan explains:

Open a telephone book at random and put a finger down blindly. Take the first syllable of the name you hit. Repeat the procedure. Link the two syllables and you have a mantra.

Mindless chanting may benefit the doer, much as speaking in tongues apparently benefited some members of the Christian Church at Corinth. But, wrote Paul, in his Corinthian letter, "I would rather speak five words with my mind . . . than ten thousand words in a tongue (1 Cor. 14:19)."

The relation of this position from the New Testament to ten thousand *mantras* should be abundantly clear.

Only Christian Meditation

Plato likened the mind of man to a ship on which the sailors had mutinied and locked the Captain below in his cabin. The task of human beings, wrote Plato, is to quell the mutiny, to release the Captain so that there can be freedom to choose a goal and work toward it consistently.

To expect that TM, or any other practice of so-called eastern meditation, which is not true meditation, will be able to quell the mutiny and give the mind real freedom is like expecting one's car doing 55 miles per hour to negotiate safely Los Angeles freeways while the driver sits on his hands, mindlessly confident that his aberrant behavior will handle the driving problem.

Mature meditation, cogitation, or steering the mind, requires much, much more. It is this *more* which prayer-meditation will give the regular practitioner in abundance. Let us now turn to the task of closing the God Gap for modern man.

The vast mass of humanity lives out its life as though there were no death and, for that matter, no God.

This is the most terrible of all disasters and the one most deserving of tears — when people who are about to die still imagine they will go on living; when, overwhelmed by miseries, they still dream of happiness; and when, in the most critical perils that surround them, they are deliriously self-assured.

— Martin Luther

Chapter 2

THE SECRET PLACE OF THUNDER

Summary Statement. The purpose here is to develop the frame of mind or the attitude necessary to create the possibility of effective prayer. Nothing can lead anyone to pray unless the basic hindrances to prayer are examined.

Is there a God? Does he hear our prayers? Does he answer our prayers? Is it God's world, the devil's, the world of a nameless power, or the world of no power except man's?

Is prayer of no value if the answer is not our answer? Are some people more gifted or more sensitive to the possibility of prayer than others? What can be given as answers to the sceptics to say what prayer is?

God

Why do people go to church? Why do you go to church? Why do you not go to church?

Each one must answer the question in his own tongue.

How does one say, GOD? In the words of W. H. Carruth:

> A fire-mist and a planet
>   A crystal and a cell,
> A jellyfish and a saurian,
>   And Caves where the cavemen dwell:
> Then a sense of law and beauty,
>   And a face turned from the clod--
> Some call it Evolution,
>   And others call it God.
>
> A picket frozen on duty--
>   A mother starved for her brood--
> Socrates drinking the hemlock,
>   And Jesus on the rood:
> And millions who, humble and nameless,
>   The straight, hard pathway trod--
> Some call it consecration
>   And others call it God.

Uncover all the human reasons. Scratch beneath the surface of all our motives. The reason we go to church is God. The faintest glimmering of God is a sign of faith — no, the Alpha and Omega of our faith. *The sign.* All our struggles are but preliminaries to go deep into the way of God, into the secret place of thunder.

The Secret Place of Thunder is a symbolic title.

The Truth

God speaks to the poet-prophet of ancient Israel, and he writes the most significant words ever expressed by man, "In the beginning God . . . (Gen. 1:1)."

God gives a vision in the temple to Isaiah, who saw the Lord sitting upon a throne, high and lifted up. He heard the seraphim sing antiphonally:

>Holy, holy, holy is the Lord of hosts:
>The whole world is full of his glory (Is.6:3)

In his heart the prophet-psalmist knows the truth, uttered by God.

>In distress you called, and I delivered you:
>I answered you in the secret place of thunder (Ps.81:7).

How has God come to you? Was it long ago? Has the idea, the vision, or the words grown dim?

How would you express the secret place of thunder of your own soul? Has he ever come to you?

No one can argue you into believing in God, but you may be given a sign. A reminder or a series of reminders of God may be given to you, today, for tomorrow and its following tomorrows.

Remember Death

Death has often been to me a sign of God.

Death took a minister-classmate of mine some years ago. An accident in the muddy bayou of a Texas town took a young boy I knew. The tail-gate of a truck snuffed out the vibrant energy of a child in a mountain town in New York State. Illness robbed a young girl in California long, long ago of her teens and lovely womanhood.

In vain do I find answers in man, in things, that for which we so frantically strive.

The sleek and deadly creatures of man's inventiveness — whether they streak into space, above our heads, or on the freeways — tell us nothing of what it means to live and to die.

What is the meaning of life?

What is the meaning of your life? Does it have any meaning at all?

Blindness

I do not know about you, but to answer such questions — indeed, to answer on some days why I get up in the morning and why it is worth it to put one foot in front of the other and then another — to answer all the basic questions, I need to push past the heavy curtains of blindness to search for the secret place of thunder.

"Blessed are those who mourn (Mt. 5:4)." The healing of the Christian's grief should be in a process of remembering rather than in a process of forgetting.

Remembering that when our loved ones were with us, God ministered to us through them. Yet our love for them was in the context of his love for us. One of us has simply outstripped the other.

"What you sow does not come to life unless it dies (I Cor.15:36)," Paul wrote.

The life for which we are truly born is to last forever. Some go before. We cannot all conveniently start together. We are soon to follow, and know where to find them.

Remember Life

Yet, life even more than death, presents signs of God.

The secret place of thunder is the mysticism of faith, the awakening of wonder, the discovery of love, the essence and beginning of all being.

It is where God grasps us, different for each of us.

It is where we discover the meaning of relationship.

Whenever we stand in the presence of a great soul, either through his writing or the reading of his biography, two things happen to us. One, what a great soul is, judges us; we have fallen so short ourselves, the possibilities of life lived greatly shrinks us and we see ourselves our real size. Two, what a great soul has, transforms us; the awe of achievement fills our hearts and we start dreaming.

Great souls both irritate and challenge. Or, stimulate and awaken.

Or, convict and heal.

Religion is Relationship

The Christian religion is not just a way of life, not just recognition of a supreme being, not even worship of the Father, Son and Holy Ghost alone. All religion so easily falls into customs, into habits and practices, into ideas and theologies or restrictions and duties.

We forget that God seeks to have us in relationship with Him, the relationship of Creator and creature.

God is the great, Great Soul. He judges and transforms.

He stimulates and awakens. He convicts and heals. He grasps.

It is the tender grasp of love. Abraham J. Heschel writes, "We must learn to abandon the view that religion is simply morality tinged with emotion. It is above all a world of its own, a private secret realm of relationship between God and man."

Mighty Acts

If our God were only a warmth of feeling, that poetic and mystical expression of emotion so commonly associated with religious piety; and if God were only the individual's motion toward mood, then all men would know God fully.

Yet, all men do not know Him. All men most certainly do not know the God of Holy Scriptures who thunders out of secret places and then moves to mountains like Sinai, and enters history through a people.

Our God acts. He reveals. Our God creates. He saves.

Our God enters human flesh. He enters our history too, yours and mine. He sanctifies. He teaches.

He loves.

He comes.

But many who would like to know God have never found Him. Perhaps, truer, they have never been ready to be found. The fault lies not with God, but with us. We are not sensitive enough.

Prayer and meditation daily and worship with fellow believers weekly at least, will gradually begin to open the closed doors of our hearts and minds to let God in.

But are there not *techniques* that can help? Basically, *no!*

Before one can talk about or utilize doing things, or techniques, one must first establish a frame of mind.

What is the frame of mind or the attitude necessary to create the possibility of effective prayer? I shall approach this question negatively, by considering the major hindrances everyone sees standing face to face with the paradox and danger and the hope and possibilities of prayer.

As a Man Thinks

One of man's first hindrances to effective prayer is to think only and always as a man thinks.

There is another way. Man has difficulty to see the other way. He would rather say that man is self-sufficient. He would rather call prayer a mere soliloquy, a self-deception, a cowardice toward life.

Now I did not indicate above that man need not think as man thinks. This is the way man is. I do not intend to write disparagingly of man's capacities. Men are extremely capable.

What I mean is that man may believe that what *he* does not think exists cannot exist. He may also believe that what *he* rejects as not being true, because *he* rejects it, it is therefore not true.

The fallacy of this reasoning is immediately evident.

Things or persons or ideas exist long before a man knows about them: chopsticks, jade, a pomegranate, a mustard seed, a friend, or God.

Man's rejection of what he does not know firsthand, or a truth presently unknown, does not invalidate them: gravity, a round world, faith, love, or prayer.

Think and Reverse It

When it comes to God and religious faith, man must take what he believes to be the truth and then reverse it. He must take it from its opposite side. This approach is sometimes given as an argument against religious faith, that it is *unreasonable*. Yet, in life, in business, in scientific experimentation — constantly, in all fields — men and women do precisely what is argued as being, in religious matters, unreasonable, taking what one believes to be the truth and then reversing it. For example, businesses often defy trends and come up with successful products. If scientists had always been *reasonable* in their research, thousands of discoveries we take for granted today would still be unknown. Yet, only when this is done in religion is it called unreasonable. Only then is it criticized.

A man must see God and religious faith contrary to the way man normally sees them, and then he will come closer to the truth. Man does not see as God sees. Man looks only on outward appearances. God looks on the heart (I Sam.16:7).

There are many arguments against prayer, which cannot be refuted by logical rebuttal. Prayer is known only by praying. Luther wrote, "No one can conceive the power of prayer except one who has tried it and learned by experience." But is this not also true in every other field? Who knows mathematics before doing mathematics? Proof comes but not at once, in prayer, mathematics, and every other area of man's endeavor.

Man can overcome this first hindrance to prayer by willingness to move himself out of the center of things. This self-centeredness blinds man even to attempt to see as God sees.

My Way, O Lord

The second hindrance man has to effective prayer is to predetermine the answers to prayer. Man's answer when he asks for things is usually, "Yes," which means that the prayer is going to be answered as he thinks it should be answered.

Or the effectiveness of prayer, as Buttrick suggests, is gauged by the answer to the shabby question: "What am I going to get out of it?" Buttrick illustrates this.

Peer Gynt boasted on his yacht that he took religion only intermittently:

> And, as one needs in days of trial
> Some certainty to place one's trust in,
> I took religion intermittently.
> That way it goes more smoothly down.
> One should not read to swallow all,
> But rather see what one has use for.

When he found himself on the beach, left a castaway, he prayed according to this pattern:

It is I, Peer Gynt! Oh, our Lord, give but heed! . .
Hear me! Let other folks' business lie over!
The world can take care of itself for the time.

He is amazed and indignant that his prayer is not answered according to his demand and exclaims:

I'm blessed if he hears me! He's deaf as his wont is!
Here's a nice thing! A God that is bankrupt of help!
Hist; I've abandoned the nigger-plantation!
And missionaries I've exported to Asia!
Surely one good turn should be worth another!
Oh, help me on board!

One thing Peer Gynt and many a soul who takes religion and prayer intermittently does not realize is that God's wrath is never greater than when He is silent. He has left us to follow our own mind and will, as we have been doing all along anyway, and do just as we please. God says, "So I gave them over to their stubborn hearts, to follow their own counsels (Ps.81:12)."

The Hard Way

Sometimes the answer to prayer is suffering. What did Jesus get out of prayer? Calvary!

Sometimes goodness cannot become contagious, religion cannot be caught, and then goodness must become sacrificial. A better way comes sometimes only by the willingness of someone to suffer.

A woman raises a good family by sacrificing her own freedom. Many a mother understands quite clearly the value of sacrificial giving. She who loses her life will find it.

We ought not determine in advance what God's answer is going to be to our prayers.

We ought also be careful for what we pray. We may get it.

Elizabeth Browning writes:

God answers sharp and sudden on some prayers,
And thrusts the thing we have prayed for in our face.
A gauntlet with a gift in't.

Wireless to Glory

The third hindrance to effective prayer is to assume that some people have naturally good radio systems to broadcast to God and fine radars to receive his message in turn, while others do not.

The gift is given to others. I am denied it. Prayer may be some souls' sincere desire still. But I have given it up because I have tried to pray but nothing has happened.

Among Christians, prayer is a little like the weather: everybody talks about it, but nobody does anything about it.

We just drift, or we learn by hit and miss. Were you ever taught to pray? Were detailed instructions beyond "Now I lay me down to sleep" given to you in a Sunday School class or in a sermon when you were a child, a young person, an adult?

All Christians can learn to pray. None are denied its benefits. The non-Christian can learn to pray, too, if he has the heart and mind to do it.

You can learn to pray.

Prayer — even just the word — is a sign of faith. It is not easy to take a sign and move to mature faith with it. Effort and struggle are required.

When you softly say, "O God," at a time of despair, it is a sign of faith.

I have approached the subject negatively, considering three major hindrances to effective prayer: (1) to think only and always as a man thinks, (2) to predetermine answers to prayer, and (3) to think that only others are sensitive enough to communicate with God.

In the beginning I asked, what is the frame of mind or the attitude necessary to create the possibility of effective prayer?

False Notions

Seeing the hindrances for what they are and overcoming them, the next question to answer seriously is, "What then is prayer?"

Forget the skeptics' answers: a healthy lie of life, auto-suggestion, rationalization, a way of swapping bribe for bribe, trade for trade. I would suggest even the rejection of some definitions suggested by Christians.

Buttrick quotes William James approvingly, that prayer is, "Intercourse with an Ideal Companion." Following this view, Buttrick himself suggests that prayer in its essence is the abiding certitude that it is comradeship with God.

God — — a companion, a comrade? This is a very popular notion, but nonetheless wrong. God is not a pal with whom we on occasion have talks, as we do with friends.

He is God! None is his equal!

Forget Your Notions

It would be better at first to forget technicalities of definitions about prayer. Prayer, like the love of God, is broader than the measures of man's mind. Something of what I have in mind was captured by James Montgomery early in the beginning of the last century:

> Prayer is the soul's sincere desire,
> Unuttered or expressed,
> The motion of a hidden fire
> That trembles in the breast.

C. S. Lewis touched the idea when he wrote of the practice of prayer without words. Lewis wrote, "I still think the prayer without words is the best — if one can achieve it."

I am really talking about dismissing, in the beginning, all notions you have had about prayer, in order to open the mind and heart to the real possibilities of relationship and communication with God, who is Creator and re-Creator, who is a Spirit, who is love, who is the redeemer of the world.

Human beings do not move toward the certitude of prayer until they have recognized the majesty and infiniteness of God, who nevertheless comes to us. God is approachable because he first approached us.

> Prayer is the burden of a sigh,
> The falling of a tear,
> The upward glancing of an eye
> When none but God is near.
>
> O thou by whom we come to God,
> The Life, the Truth, the Way,
> The path of prayer thyself hast trod:
> Lord, teach us how to pray.

Ignorance and stupidity are always related to other people, not to ourselves. Think of the ways many approach a new idea or a problem. Five steps:

1. Resist it just on general principles. It makes one think. Do not want to think. Against thinking.

2. Do not want to hear what is said when idea or problem is being explained.

3. Do not want to hear what is said when idea or problem is being explained the second time.

4. Do not want to hear what is said when idea or problem is being explained the third time.

5. Now that the idea or problem has been explained three times, become experts and authorities on what has neither been heard nor understood by explaining why idea or problem has been rejected.

Such people always block every good thing. Of course – not *you!*

Let us now turn to another kind of problem about the Christian life and prayer: making up our minds.

JEREMIAH 5

³⁰ An appalling and horrible thing
    has happened in the land:
³¹ the prophets prophesy falsely,
    and the priests rule at their direction;
my people love to have it so,
    but what will you do when the end
    comes?

Chapter 3

BEGINNING A LIFE OF DEEPER COMMITMENT

Summary Statement. The purpose here is to treat how to begin a life of deeper commitment. There are many reluctances to face. We would rather not change. Honesty is required. Faith as a word and as belief must be examined, in this examination tackling all the unnatural views that normally are held about the religious life and religious faith.

For example, many believe that a person has to move into unnatural and unreasoning patterns of action and thought to understand the things of the spirit.

Commitment also involves expansion of thought and life of what a way of prayer means. Certain basic principles make up a full and rounded life of prayer. These will be presented and analyzed.

Be Honest

You would like to learn to pray.

Yet, you still have many questions. You are not fully convinced that you want to undertake this discipline. However, if you believe that you are fairly well convinced, then answer this question: How much time, attention, and energy are you willing to give?

Start your answer to this question by being thoroughly honest. Perhaps one or more of the following would constitute an honest answer:

1. I want to do this if it is not too demanding.
2. I am willing to give some time and effort, but unless I get immediate results I will not go on.
3. I have needs and have tried everything else so I might just as well try prayer.
4. I feel a little embarrassed about the thought of praying because I associate prayer with saints and holy people or with a few pious frauds I know who are anything but saints.
5. Since prayer involves Bible reading, I have tried reading the Bible in the past, unsuccessfully, so I have doubts as to whether I can overcome all

my hesitancies. I am not even sure that I have the spiritual and academic background to understand prayer and what the Bible is really all about.

Do any of the above five answers, or possibly all five, reflect your honest appraisal of your present frame of mind and attitude? Perhaps you have other feelings and objections. Write them down. It is important that you list them.

Your Definition of Faith

Now, with your honest feelings and objections before you, ask yourself what meaning you attach to the word *faith*. Is your definition of *faith* believing in something you know is not true? Or, is your definition of *faith* believing in something you are fairly sure of but at the same time a little skeptical? Do you believe in God, yet at the same time also disbelieve, sometimes?

When Jesus heard the plea of the father to cure his sick boy, Jesus said, "All things are possible to him who believes (Mk. 9:23)."

Immediately the father cried out and said, "I believe, help my unbelief (Mk. 9:24)."

The father was very much like you and me. He was troubled and had a need. His son was very sick. Are we just as honest as this father was? *He admitted both his faith and doubt, the twofold tension that was built into his faith — belief and unbelief.* This tension is *normal* to every person, though it is experienced differently according to a person's background and training.

Two Kinds of Believing

If you can be *that* honest — a necessary prerequisite to any venture into the spiritual world — you are ready to begin. You may not be fully honest about everything, yet if you are even only partially honest, count on it that you are ready. You are normal, hopeful while also being partially apprehensive and somewhat skeptical. Doubt may even be dominant.

However, you must go on. There are two kinds of believing. The first kind of believing is assent to something: I believe that what is said about God is true. This is more a form of knowledge than the genuine faith which God demands.

The second kind of believing is where you put your trust in God, give yourself up to thinking that you can have dealings with Him, and that He will do what He has promised.

Of this second kind of believing or faith, Martin Luther writes, "Such faith, which throws itself upon God, whether in life or death, alone makes a Christian man (woman)."

Most of us fail to grow into this faith of which Luther writes because we do not test it to prove what is the will of God.

Moving From Your Faith

One of your tasks in the weeks ahead, assuming that you will at least go far enough to do some testing, will be to exercise your mind and spirit to see whether or not *faith is able to give proof of the power of God and proof of the power and practice of your faith, the faith God will give you, in your life and deeds.*

The definition of faith given by the writer of *Hebrews* is a good one: "Now faith is the assurance of things hoped for, the conviction of things not seen (Heb. 11:1)."

Yet this definition for many people is interpreted as going it blind, going on in a hopeless sort of way, wishing rather than believing, and therefore a negation of reason, really destructive and not constructive in building faith.

What the writer of *Hebrews* is saying is that he recognizes the genuine existence and reality of truth that cannot be touched with the hands alone. Love for someone else is like that.

You have a feeling for a husband, a wife, or a child. The feeling is quite intangible and invisible. An idea is not able to be touched with the hands either. But it can be perceived or grasped with the spirit and/or the mind. Certainly, we act on such love that we have for members of that family and are willing to work to test an idea *before* any proof is given. Is that not true for *you*? You act before proof?

The writer of *Hebrews* does not say faith is contrary to reason, but he implies that there are things hoped for and convictions about things not seen that are above or beyond one's present and immediate understanding of reason.

Being Unnatural

Most of us have erroneous views about *faith. Faith,* as a word or as an experience, may grow in our understanding. Faith must be tested to have such growth.

All of us have erroneous views about Prayer and Bible reading. Therefore, test your present faith. Take the partial and incomplete faith you now have in Prayer and Bible reading and test that faith. See what happens. Note the results. Take it step by step, just as you do everything else in life you have ever learned.

Overcome the notion so prevalent when it comes to all matters that we call spiritual or religious, that a person has to move into unnatural and unreasoning patterns of action and thought to understand the things of the spirit.

All Learning Is Alike

The typist never learns to type until he is taught or teaches himself and utilizes the same concentration, the same work, and the same general skills that must be exercised to bake a cake, make gravy, or repair a broken chair. All learning is alike.

Be assured that the steps you are taking here follow that which is normal and natural as in any other area in the beginning stages.

Naturally, as you progress you will develop skills and insights that are peculiar to prayer, but these will also follow natural growth patterns.

The Death of the Churches

God cannot die. *The true Church cannot die either.* Yet, the churches could die if you and I, along with millions of others, do not now embark on this prayer/venture of faith and understanding.

Forces have captured the churches today which could destroy the genuine life of the true church in them.

Look at Church History

Throughout the history of the Christian Church, in every age, the Church has always faced the dangers of apathy, apostasy, and heresy. These dangers were often brought into the Church by the very leaders who claimed to be saving the Church.

Popes, Bishops, priests, ministers, and lay people have often fostered destructiveness of the true Church mainly because they have been motivated by personal selfishness.

None can deny that today the churches face daily losses.

Behind the Times

The churches have always been slow to adjust to changing times. Changes in society the past fifty years have been more radical and revolutionary than in any other age. The Churches have neither directed nor adequately judged any of these forces. Rather, they seem to have adapted themselves either to resist change or adjust too readily to secularism.

In your personal search for faith and deepening of your prayer life, you must at all times keep alive the fact that you are engaged in an effort which cannot be considered apart from the life of the Church and of other Christians.

In what follows, in dealing with certain basic assumptions about the Christian and his prayer life, you will discover each assumption will support you to develop further motivation, resolve, and staying power in this venture.

The Bible and God's Word

First, however, it is important to recognize that there are certain values in substituting the words *God's Word* for *Bible*. Or, they may be equated.

The reason for this is that a person may read the Bible without finding in it *God's Word.* You will be seeking to discover in prayer and by praying not just words in the Bible, but *God's Word.*

All such persons read the words of the Bible but experience no revelation, even though the words they read still are the vehicle through which *God's Word* is revealed.

Prior to recording of the words was the Creative Spirit of God. I am not talking primarily about symbolism in the words or even mysticism: "In the beginning was the Word (Jn.1:1)."

For the moment then, since this will come up later in various ways many times, let me say only that from now on your thoughts and attention should be directed to coming to know the Living God who has revealed Himself in and through a book we call the *Bible*.

What that kind of revelation must be called is *God's Word*. At the moment you may only be able to read the words and not fully comprehend what they mean — *God's Word*. However, by continuing in this study you will come fully to understand this truth through personally experiencing *God's Word*.

Certain Basic Assumptions

Earlier I suggested dismissing, in the beginning, all notions you have had about prayer. The purpose of this was to suggest that *most* notions, or ideas, held about prayer simply are not true. You must unlearn before you can learn.

Now, with this open mind, I suggest certain basic assumptions for your consideration to come to know fully and understand genuine Christian prayer. Religion involves prayer. Not all prayer is valid. Today we must speak of false and true prayer. Observe the following practices:

* Try to understand God's Word every day,

* Pray all the time.

* Think all the time.

* Be sensitive to new insights.

* Pray naturally and freely.

* Use written prayers.

* Act out your conclusions.

* Worship regularly.

* Work in the world.

As should now be clear, prayer is not a certain form or pious words. Prayer and God's word are inseparable.

Prayer is an all-encompassing way of life.

Blessed Lord, who hast caused all holy Scriptures to be written for our learning; grant that we may in such wise hear them, read, mark, learn, and inwardly digest them, that by patience and comfort of Thy holy Word, we may embrace, and ever hold fast, the blessed hope of everlasting life, which Thou hast given us in our Savior Jesus Christ. Amen.

This prayer, *called Collect,* used the Second Sunday in Advent, is a 1549 prayer, reflecting the new interest of the Reformation in acquainting the people with the contents and teachings of the Bible.

The secularism that pervades the American consciousness is essentially . . . thinking and living in terms of a framework of reality and value remote from the religious beliefs simultaneously professed.

This is at least part of the picture presented by religion in contemporary America . . . men and women valuing the Bible as revelation, purchasing and distributing it by the millions, yet apparently seldom reading it themselves.

-- Will Herberg

Chapter 4

THE UNKNOWN BOOK

Summary Statement: The purpose here is to treat the use of the Bible in the development of maturity of prayer life. It must be noted that many people believe the Bible is very important, yet have little knowledge of the Bible, though no one ever knows why it is important. Few take the time to read it *daily.* A second stress is to get the learner to realize that the Bible is "holy writing," that is, the books are inspired, and that God has a way of speaking through this Word.

The Bible must be read in a devotional way. The reader must ask for the guidance of the Holy Spirit and to expect that, from time to time, he will hear God speaking from its pages in words clearly addressed to his own needs.

Important But Ignored

Few people, if any, would contradict the judgment that the Bible has molded the inner character of our public institutions, inspired high achievement in literature and art, ennobled the language of our daily life, and has been and is the guide and companion of millions of persons.

We nod in assent. The Bible is truly a lamp unto our feet.

However, there is a vast difference in what we may believe and what response we make to that belief.

Do you read and use the Bible daily?

Some would answer, "No, I do not."

Others might answer, "Yes, sometimes, but I would like to read and use the Bible more than I do."

Perhaps many today would fall into the category of one of the characters in Marc Connelly's play *Green Pastures.* After hearing the reading of a portion of the Bible, a woman exclaims to the minister, "Oh, Mr. Deshee, I thinks it's jes' wonderful. I cain't understand any of it!"

These are jarring words. These are sad words. These are true words in revealing where many people stand.

The Bible to many is largely an unknown and mysterious set of books. It is presumably the source of our spiritual life, yet hidden. It contains great principles, yet these are known only second hand. Firsthand knowledge is rare.

In a day of revolution in our land because few act like neighbors, Biblical thought — truly heard, read, marked, learned, and inwardly digested — could change the nation.

A Practical Suggestion

Let me be very practical in terms of your life and in terms of Christian Churches throughout America. I am going to suggest that all Christians ought to be encouraged, assisted, and trained to read and use the Bible.

I realize that this is a simple suggestion, too plain, too obvious, and too unvarnished. Rather, I should propose some complicated and profound-sounding theory. I should propose that Christians read and use material *about* the Bible before reading it.

Is it not being too ambitious to hope that you and other Christians could be challenged by such a radical idea?

Resistance to Use of the Bible

The actual text of the Bible is remote, too complicated, and far beyond the capacities of the majority of the people, is what one would hear. This is the first objection.

The arguments are just beginning. Resistance is even now stiffening in your mind. Hear the arguments because they might sound like some you have already used against the idea of reading the Bible on a daily basis. They should be out in the open.

Some scholars are critical about Christian members reading and using the Bible — — on the grounds that this would be placing a dangerous weapon in the hands of untrained people.

The argument is ages old. It was held in the middle ages. It was shouted against the reformers in the 16th Century. The argument is held today by many educators. The common element in all these is a pernicious doctrine called *specialization.*

The 16th Century Bible translator, William Tyndale, once remarked to a learned man, a foe of his efforts to place the Holy Scriptures in a language understood by the people, "I will so bring it about that the boy at the plough's tail shall know more of the Bible than thou dost." For his efforts, Tyndale was martyred in 1536.

The Holy Scriptures are available today in every modern language. Yet the old fight must be waged.

Resistance From Scholars

Among the critics would have to be numbered many Christian Biblical scholars, who warn that no one should read a single verse of the Bible before mastering Hebrew, Greek, Aramaic, Latin, and Sanscrit. After that, one must master and thoroughly digest the Apocrypha and Pseudepigrapha.

Unfortunately, some Christian clergy make such a fetish over the original languages they frighten people out of independent Bible study and, incidentally, think of themselves more highly than they ought to think.

Among the critics would also have to be placed everyone who says sincerely, "I do not know enough to read and use the Bible."

To all these and to many others it should be pointed out that we live in an age of specialization. Gone is the jack-of-all-trades. Gone or going is the family doctor. Gone or going is the family pastor. Each one of us is being trained by the climate of our day not to see, feel, and understand the broad sweep of life.

American people apparently no longer place a premium on common sense. We would rather have our psychoses, or disturbances because we lack psychoses, our ailments, or our maladjustments — described in ten dollar words with fees to match — than to be people called upon to redeem mankind from splintered living.

God Cares For You

Do not misunderstand me. I would not wish fully to return to an earlier age. Specialization, when properly controlled, gives us vast benefits.

What I am objecting to is the specialization that has invaded even the personal life, the area of personal decision. We seek causes outside of ourselves, something on which to blame our predicaments, anything that will ease our minds and consciences for the lack of individual responsibility and individuality. We have lost respect for ourselves and our dignity, under God, who created us a little lower than the angels.

Your life is tremendously significant. Your influence may lead your family or your friends aright to redirect them properly. Your thoughts, your feelings, your insights, and your life are all precious. You are important. *God cares for you.*

All of these ideas are Biblical ideas that have entered into the warp and woof of our lives and in society.

Are we going to throw them away by neglect? What a terrible day that will be!

Famine in the Land

Withdraw the power from which they stem, God through His revelation of Himself and His will through Holy Scriptures, and we will have a famine.

The prophet Amos once had a vision of a people without the word of the Lord:

"Behold, the days are coming," says the Lord God, "when I will send famine on the land; not a famine of bread, nor a thirst for water, but of hearing the words of the Lord. They shall wander from sea to sea, and from north to east; they shall run to and fro, to seek the word of the Lord, but they shall not find it. (Amos 8:11-12)."

The Bible is bread, feeding our hunger. The Bible is water, quenching our thirst. When the word of the Lord is inwardly digested, our grasp of the broad sweep of God's meaning for all men crumbles the petty specializations of men. The psalmist says that the Lord brought him forth into a broad place, when He came to him (Ps. 18:19).

Are we then afraid to have our limitations broken? Are we afraid of the vision of a people standing against the might of godless men? Of what are we afraid, the instilling of hope and faith, of responsibilities, of the creative power of the Almighty God who can make all things new?

The Fearful Clergy

Of what are the clergy of America afraid if their people inwardly digest the Word of the Lord?

These men of God know the long road of discipline. They are aware of the difficulties of Biblical interpretation, realizing how easy it is to go astray. Do they fear for their people: the anxieties and discouragements that will come to live by faith? Do not the clergy know that no casual or half-hearted effort will be of value but only lifelong dedication?

Perhaps these men of God have specialized too long. None of the above objections or fears are valid. They may be warning signals but they are not stop signs.

I say to you that the course ahead, for those who seek the Word of the Lord, is hard. It is easier not to think. It is easier to seek the specialist in religious thought and have him give the answers and accept these answers than to search Holy Scriptures one's self.

If this argument is believed and practiced, America is dead.

Hold Back

If, then, the difficulties are accepted, two major problems would have to be grappled with, the first being that of the hesitancy produced in us by Biblical specialists.

Begin simply. There is reason to be more concerned about the things we do understand in the Bible than about the things we do not understand, an observation said to have been made once by Mark Twain.

Several verses of Scripture might point this up for us.

Paul writes to the Galatians: "Let us have no self-conceit, no provoking of one another, no envy of one another (5:26)," and, later, "For if any one thinks he is something, when he is nothing, he deceives himself (6:3)."

Do you understand these verses? Do they speak of human problems? A problem you have? Suppose these words were not only heard, read, marked and learned but also *inwardly digested;* would they not guide the disciples of Christ?

Take another passage from Galatians: "For neither circumcision counts for anything, nor uncircumcision, but a new creation (6:15)."

Here is a more difficult passage but not beyond understanding, especially when your knowledge of the whole of the Bible gradually increases and if a guiding paragraph or two of explanation is included on the day you would read this passage.

This Is The Secret

Problem passages of scripture, what about them? Few of them are beyond understanding. Most respond to understanding when *inwardly digested.* Some few passages may remain enigmas. Even daily life gives us a few tough things to understand, but we do not normally drop all of life because of them. Why do it with the Bible?

The biggest difficulties for the Bible reader are (1) to accept the fact that God exists, (2) that He speaks through the Scriptures, (3) that He speaks to us in our day, and (4) that He speaks to you.

The Old Testament book of Daniel and the New Testament book of Revelation create real problems. No one can deny this. But, add to these some other chapters, you still have left a preponderance of material to read that opens wide doors of understanding into faith and grace and justification and problems of living.

Is Man Free?

The second major problem that any person has to read and use the Bible is not limited to church folk in the pews. This difficulty is also a stumbling block to everyone: the scholar, the scientist, the clergyman, the educator, the politician, the housewife, the businessman, and the young student.

What is that problem? *The submission of the will to read with an open and free mind.*

The Will Is a Stumbling Block

Paul writes about all men when he states:

"I do not understand my own actions. For I do not do what I want, but I do the very thing I hate (Romans 7:15)."

"I can will what is right, but I cannot do it. For I do not do the good I want, but the evil I do not want is what I do (Romans 7:18-19)."

St. Augustine writes, "A man's free will, indeed, avails for nothing except to sin, if he knows not the way of truth."

Martin Luther writes, "For our will is the greatest power within us, and we must pray against it: my Father, suffer me not to have my will. Oppose my will and break it . . . only let Thy will and not mine be done."

Back of Paul's, St. Augustine's, and Luther's observations is the belief that God has given man a free will. Why then does not man let it remain free? Why does man make it his own will?

Finding Genuine Freedom

Unruly people rule America because Christians have not submitted their wills to God's will. None truly knows his neighbor because his will is not free.

Freedom to use our free wills comes from hearing, reading, marking, learning, and inwardly digesting the Holy Scriptures. Only then do we experience and respond to the love of God through Christ Jesus. God's love alone cures the perverseness of our own wills.

God's Word

Let me summarize. The Bible is the most wonderful book in the world, but few people read it. The major hindrance today of thorough study of the Bible is presented by the exponents of the doctrine of specialization. I have dealt largely with specialization because it looms so large over our lives, warping and hindering our motivation to open the pages of the Word of the Lord. I have made the suggestion that all Christians in all Christian Churches in America ought to be encouraged, assisted and trained to read and use the Bible.

One final question: why bother to make the effort?

The Bible is not just like any other literature or history. The Bible is the record of the revelation of God Himself in history.

God's Word is a living Word.

God makes use of the Word to speak directly to the ear and conscience.

As *God's Word* is heard, read, marked, learned, and inwardly digested it can be expected that the Christian believer will hear God speaking from its pages in words clearly addressed to his own needs.

Prayer and meditative reflection added to the reading of God's Word daily amount to talking to God, thinking through His will, *chewing* the thoughts of God.

Not abnormal, not strange.

Most natural.

Most wonderful.

No man has a right to lead such a life of
contemplation as to forget . . . the service
due to his neighbor; nor has any man a
right to be so immersed in active life as
to neglect the contemplation of God.

—St. Augustine

The God Gap

by

George Nelson Thompson

BOOK 2

JEREMIAH 29

11 For I know the plans I have for you, says the LORD, plans for welfare and not for evil, to give you a future and a hope. 12 Then you will call upon me and come and pray to me, and I will hear you. 13 You will seek me and find me; when you seek me with all your heart, 14 I will be found by you, says the LORD.

Louis Cassels, Senior Editor and Religion Writer for United Press International (UPI), died early in 1974 at the age of 52. Cassels' religious columns were always cogent, reflecting his own Christian commitment. What follows is one of Louis Cassels' helpful columns.

HAPPENING OR HABIT?

Many people believe acts of religious devotion are more sincere and meaningful if they're entirely spontaneous.

That's debatable.

Spontaneity of religious expression undoubtedly has one great advantage: it guards us against the hypocrisy of doing things, such as going to church, because we're expected to, and against the sterility of doing things, such as saying grace before meals, out of sheer habit.

But those who engage in acts of worship only when they feel "in the mood" are disregarding the example of Jesus, the teaching of the Bible, and the experience of a long line of saints.

Jesus treasured spontaneous acts of devotion.   But he knew a person's mood may be affected by many things, such as illness, fatigue, or adversity. He also knew it is precisely in such low moments that human beings most need to turn to God for comfort and guidance. So he set an example of disciplined regularity in worship.

From what he did as well as what he taught, we know Jesus believed in attending worship services every Sabbath. He also set aside time for private prayer and meditations every day.

The Bible reflects the same viewpoint, especially in the letters of St. Paul. Paul admonished members of early Christian communities to be "constant" - i.e.- regular- in prayer. No one knew better than Paul how easy it is to become so distracted by other concerns - not just frivolous pleasures but important duties - that one never feels "in the mood" to take time out for quiet communion with God. So he insisted that regular periods must be set aside - and kept inviolate - for prayer and meditation.

Many great saints, such as St. Francis and St. Teresa of Avila, often went through spells of "dryness" when they felt absolutely devoid of any spontaneous devotion to God. But they learned from experience that perseverance in worship when you least feel like it is an act of pure obedience, a deliberate subjection of your own will to God's will.

Another reason for regularity in prayer, Bible reading, and church attendance is that you never can tell, in advance, when some word, sentence, or incident will suddenly illuminate your mind and lift up your spirit. It can happen, unexpectedly, unforeseeably, in the midst of dullest sermons, or during private devotions which you had to drive yourself to make.

Spontaneity is a fine thing, and there is merit to the contention of Pentecostals and young people in the Jesus movement that there ought to be room for spontaneous acts of worship in church services. But the testimony of Jesus and the saints is that most spontaneous upwellings of love for God are most likely to occur in the context of lives ruled by a discipline of daily devotion.

Reprinted by Permission of United Press International.

The Bible ought to be read not with a blank, pious look, not with a rejection of one's present life situation.

Read the Bible with the mind full of the walking, working, urgent, and pressing problems which surround you.

Prayer For Guidance

Blessed Lord, who hast caused all holy Scriptures to be written for our learning; Grant that we may in such wise hear them, read, mark, learn, and inwardly digest them, that by patience and comfort of thy holy Word, we may embrace, and ever hold fast, the blessed hope of everlasting life, which thou hast given us in our Savior Jesus Christ. Amen.

—1549 A.D.

INTRODUCTION

APPROACHING THE DAILY TASK

Summary Statement. The purpose here is to treat the mechanics of prayer practically. There are many varieties of approaches. Here, one common approach has been chosen. Step by step the learner is guided and initiated into the necessary habits to make prayer a way of life.

There will be a review of some of the key points considered earlier, particularly the area of will power. How is the will directed? What is discipline? There is included an examination of the reasons that will be ever-present daily for everyone. The reasons are why one should *not* continue the daily practice of prayer.

What should one expect to happen as a result of daily prayer? What are the special problems and distractions? How does one recognize the signs of growth and new life and encourage these?

A *sevenfold pattern* is given for guidance:

1. Settle in
2. Read the Bible passages
3. Ponder the Reading
4. Reflect again
5. Pray
6. The Lord's Prayer
7. Your Written Thoughts

Time of Day

Choose for your daily devotions a time of day which can be constant in a place where you will not be disturbed. No matter how little time you do spend, keep in mind a goal which ranges between five minutes and one hour, or more. Martin Luther, it has been said, often spent three hours daily in prayer.

The time of day is important. You will have to determine this on the basis of your work and other habits of living. Many report that the morning hours seem best. Of course any time of day will be valuable.

One big argument often given for the period shortly after rising is that the body and mind are rested and the mind is more open. Many also report another value: the time of day *before* activities or work absorb them completely. Instead of allowing the influences of the day to determine one's actions and important decisions, God is given greater priority to help determine the actions of the day.

It is a personal matter whether this period, if it is after rising, be scheduled before or after breakfast.

What then do you do?

What You Will Need

Sit at a desk or a table where you are able to place your books and writing material. You should have at least these items:

A Bible.

A Dictionary.

A pad for writing and a pen or pencil.

A devotional guide.

The above are the necessities. Later, you may wish to add a Bible commentary, a Bible dictionary, more than one translation of the Bible (other than the one you have chosen), a Bible concordance, and one of the classic books of written prayers. You ought to be on the lookout for other devotional guides, keeping in mind the characteristics of such a daily guide which you conclude are best for you.

There are varieties of approaches to daily prayer, as suggested earlier. You will no doubt eventually grow into your own, which probably will be a composite of different patterns you will read about, your own needs, and (very important) your own discoveries of what works for you. You will experiment. John Wesley*, the great English evangelist and founder of Methodism, spoke frequently about "the experimental knowledge of God." You will naturally be doing your own experimenting.

Until that time comes, unless you already have a plan which is satisfactory for you, a common approach is this *sevenfold pattern* which now will be presented.

Settle In

Settle in means getting into the proper frame of body and mind for your private devotions. There is no way suitable for everyone to learn how this should be done. Be sure of this, though, that when you are trying to start, it will be far more difficult than when you have had some experience at *settling in.*

Adjust your chair. Get a drink of water. Make a telephone call. Check something in the newspaper. Let the dog in and the cat out. On and on.

As you sit, wherever it is, you might try *not* crossing your legs. Sit comfortably in the chair, feet on the floor, body relaxed, arms on the table.

The eight-volume Journal of John Wesley (1703-1791) may well accompany Bible reading and daily meditation. It has been calculated that in 50 years of ministry Wesley traveled 250,000 miles, mostly on horseback, and preached more than 40,000 sermons.

Allow your thoughts normally and naturally to flow, directing them to your purpose. What is your purpose? *Oh yes, prayer, Bible, concentration* - let your thinking relax, your mind wander - *this is new to me, what are you supposed to do, this seems silly, never prayed before, now, that is an embarrassing thought.* All thought is proper. There simply is no right or wrong about your wanderings from one subject to another.

Gradually, then decisively, you might begin by praying the Lord's Prayer. You have *settled in.* You will do better tomorrow, better the next day, especially as you begin thoughtfully to analyze what you must do better to *settle in.*

Read the Bible Passages

For each day there will be given Bible passages for reading. Some people find it helpful to have memorized the books of the Bible in the order in which they are placed in each of the Testaments. This makes it easier, for example, to know that Psalms is about in the middle of the Old Testament and Hebrews is toward the end of the New Testament.

The important principle, however, is simply to look for the book. If you are asked to read Gen. 5:1-5, you turn to Genesis, the 5th chapter, and read verses 1 through 5. The colon (:) separates the chapter from the verses.

Another example might look like this: Jer. 5:4-6, 12-15. This means the book of Jeremiah, the 5th chapter, verses 4 through 6, then jump to verse 12 and read verses 12 through 15.

One more example: Rom. 14:1-5, 20-15:1-2. This means the New Testament book of Romans, the 14th chapter, verses 1 through 5, then skip to verse 20 and read through to the end of chapter 14 and go on to chapter 15, reading the first two verses.

Read the passages indicated meditatively, that is, thoughtfully, slowly, deliberately, reflecting carefully over each verse and word for the meaning of the whole passage. Pause if a thought strikes you, or you do not understand the words. Reread.

Ponder the Reading

Take the time, then, to turn over the ideas and meanings which seem clear to you. Consider again those words or ideas which are unclear. Try to determine their meaning.

Suddenly, you may remember a telephone call you should make and a letter which must be written that day. Take the time, immediately, to write down a memo to yourself to do those things, then return to your meditation of the passages of the Bible you have just read. Drop all recollection of the phone call and letter.

In the beginning do not be overly concerned with complete understanding of any passage in the Bible, but you may simply ask yourself, "What is God saying here? Is He saying anything to me?"

In the last passage mentioned reference was made to Rom. 14:1-5, 20-15:1-2. Chapter 15:1 read, "We who are strong ought to bear with the failings of the weak, and not to please ourselves . . . "

A reflective meditation about this passage might go like this: *. . mmm . . . strange advice . . . weaklings ought to take care of themselves . . . I am going to please myself before putting up with some weak guy . . . I worked hard to get where I am . . . do not agree at all . . . (long pause, the mind racing to a thousand ideas) . . . Jim physically was stronger than I was in school wrestling . . . he helped me . . . lot of time too, helping me make the team . . . never would have without him . . . Uncle John gave Alice and me a lift when Billy had his bad accident . . .*

It is not difficult to see what careful deliberate reflection can do, forcing an evaluation of past experiences and making one realize that, in fact, the help from others in the past had been completely forgotten, that one's position today was a selfish one, and the two were in contradiction. Revision might be in order.

Read Devotional Guide

The same approach as just stated above applies in reading the devotional guide for the day.

Keep in mind making notes when thoughts occur, even to small items which might need to be picked up from the store. But, immediately return to the meditation.

Reflect Again

You might wish either to read the passages through once again, or just take the time to reflect meditatively on the total contents of the Bible and the devotional guide. Not always will they deal exactly with the same theme. That is not necessary. Concepts and relationships are pictures which might form later in the day, or the next week.

The important point here is that you have taken time *out* of your day to think the thoughts of God out of His Word and a man's thoughtful opinion about these words.

Reread the last sentence. Note the stress made on the word *out*. This is called to your attention now. Later, when you come to the view that now that your personal devotions are over and you go to your work you may feel that you must take time *out* of your day with God to do some necessary secular tasks. Reversed.

8

Then, later still, God ... devotions, secular work, errands, telephone calls, letters, relationships ... all of these are not *out* of anything but a whole. Life is together.

Pray

What has been going on all along has been a form of prayer. Prayer cannot be so completely isolated from thoughts and meditation. Reflective meditations are prayers of a sort. They are not just talking to yourself. You *may* just be talking to yourself, but if your sensitivity is high enough you may begin to realize that your "talking" is *praying to God*.

To pray, however, is separated in this sequence to point out that at some point you must begin to formulate in words, or thought-words, communications to God. It is not that He needs to be told your thoughts. He already knows them. You need to word them to know where you stand.

Close your eyes. Who is God? Who are you? What is God's will for you?

O God of all the earth, almighty, I am thy servant, help me to know Thy (your is just as holy) *will. Guide me to do your will. In Jesus' name. Amen.*

The above prayer might be halting, not in the best literary style, but it is *your* prayer. You started. You will grow.

The Lord's Prayer

You may wish to close with the Lord's Prayer. Memorized or written prayers have great values. No one tires of hearing a good story repeated. Children like to hear the same bedtime story repeated over and over again.

The Lord's Prayer has been considered the perfect prayer.

Has it ever occurred to you that Jesus' response to his disciples' request, "Teach us to pray" came out of his own early prayer efforts? Possibly beginning in his childhood, Jesus over a period of many years haltingly, just as we do, prayed and then, as Luke states, after questioning the teachers in the temple, "Jesus increased in wisdom and in stature, and in favor with God and man (Lk. 2:52)."

Out of Jesus' long meditations over many years, when he was in his thirties he told his disciples how to pray because he was no stranger to developing patterns of prayer.

Use of Imagination

Say that a woman plans a dinner. She projects her thoughts to the occasion of the dinner. What will I serve? How will I prepare it? What will the evening be like? Whom should I invite?

In answering these and other questions, she takes certain specific steps toward putting the dinner party together. However, she is guided in each step by her imagination as she had earlier reconstructed the whole evening.

The same wholeness in imagination might also be said to guide the person who utilized a pattern of daily devotions. Worship and adoration of Almighty God is his basic aim. From worship and adoration of Almighty God he expects his whole life - mind, feeling, and actions - to be changed.

To put it another way, he reads the Bible in a mood of prayer and meditation - imaginatively - and he prays in a mood of work. For in praying the Christian is doing, in part, his work as a Christian.

All of the seven steps are a whole. Each is related to the other.

Each day that this pattern is followed builds a week, then a regularity every week which aids the next day's period of daily devotion.

Eventually the time will come when all the hours of every day, whether awake or sleep, become infused with the power and will of God.

Your Written Thoughts

Earlier it was suggested that you write down thoughts which came to you during reading, meditating, and praying. The importance of this listing now must be explained.

Let us go back to the first step, *settle in.* Each day as you begin to *settle in* make it a habit to review your notes from previous days. Some things have been done. Some will take longer. Some will embarrass you. Some will vex you. Some will frustrate you.

These are your private promptings. Obviously, you may say, I do not need God's help to make a telephone call. This is done. You cross it off the list. But, suppose it is a difficult telephone call, requiring the asking of another for forgiveness? You can take that problem into your prayers. You may discover what is impossible for you to do, with God's help is now possible. The fact is, you could not make even a simple telephone call, or breathe, without God's help. None of us can.

From my own experience I can report that for many months I have had "problems" on my list of "things to do," prompted by my meditations and coming out of the reading of God's Words. Eventually, when I have given up on myself I have discovered that God has not given up on me. The "problems" get answered, some quite miraculously, eventually.

This thought process of remembering, or of bringing out of one questions or new ideas, can only be called the prompting of the Holy Spirit. Questioning is seeking the guidance of the Holy Spirit, knowing patiently that not all neglect can be made up for overnight. Not that God needs the time, but we do to catch up with Him and His plans for us.

Often those future plans are not revealed to us *until* that which is obviously near, which might be distasteful, gets done first. Then, the next step is revealed by God.

Distractions

Many books on prayer deal with the subject of distractions. The obvious ones - noise in the street, the wrong place to be for one's meditations or the wrong time - can be handled easily. You change the situation.

However, to many the main distractions are things like anger or having evil and unclean thought and desires coming, even in the middle of praying.

Relax. Do not resort to will power. Make such distractions the center of your attention, your prayer-attention, your "problem" for God to handle.

By persistence you will discover over and over again, more than coincidentally, that the Bible passages for *that day* deal with your "problem."

Even angry feelings toward God ought be expressed. You might honestly for the first time find yourself talking to Him. Your "distractions" might, for the first time, become problems solved.

Four Things To Do

—recognize that God will lead you.

—prepare to expect the unexpected.

—prepare to expect the expected.

—adjust to both the unexpected and the expected.

The Main Task

Yet in all of this doing which has been the entire thrust of this chapter, remember that the major purpose of your praying is not to do things or to have things happen to you.

The main task is the unceasing praise of God and adoration of Him. The doing of things or having things happen to you are only by-products of this main task of the worshipping Christian.

By keeping this in mind, you may confidently expect doors to open to foster your activity in doing.

No matter how much you are taught to do, how much is revealed to you, you still stand in the presence of the mysteries of God.

Revelation will lead to further appreciation of the mystery of God, on and on for the rest of your days: mystery to revelation to mystery to revelation, always being faced with the necessity to act by faith toward the continuing wonderful mystery of God.

PSALM 18

30 This God—his way is perfect;
   the promise of the LORD proves true;
   he is a shield for all those who take
   refuge in him.

THE FIRST WEEK
HOW FIRM A FOUNDATION

Introductory Bible reading for this week:
Psalms 104:1-13

"In the beginning God," the opening words of the book of Genesis, are remarkable. One could contemplate their significance for a lifetime and not exhaust their meaning.

Equally remarkable are the words of the evangelists about Jesus' resurrection: "He is risen!"

These sets of words are intimately related to each other. They encompass God's plan for each of us and for His Church.

God laid the foundations of the world. God also daily continues His creative process. God creates. God cares. God saves.

Genesis is a book of faith. It presents beginnings of theological themes which culminate in the New Testament. How firm a foundation!

* * * * *

Remember!

1. Read the Bible passages first.
2. Read, then, the meditation for each day.
3. Do *not* read more than one meditation each day. Spiritual growth cannot be hurried.
4. Take notes of thoughts you may have. Follow up daily as many of these as is reasonable.
5. Answer the questions which follow each daily meditation.
6. Occasionally you may wish to review the chapter you have just read.

Do these things and God will be with you!

1st Day — More Than Forever

Colossians 1:11-20

The mind should be staggered by thinking of the beginning and the end of time. If it is not, it is not a thinking mind.

Scientists report to us that every new discovery of man only reveals, first, how little is known about life, the world, and what today we speak of as "outer space." Second, the unfolding of a mystery produces many more mysteries.

God has chosen to show man important elements of His plan through the Holy Scriptures. None is more significant than what He tells us about Jesus Christ. He was with God "in the beginning." That means that Christ is eternal, while also being a true man. Are you baffled? Would it be better to remain in ignorance than to have to fathom such a mystery?

There are many people who say about Christ, "I cannot understand Him or the Scriptures; therefore, I will not believe."

From simple to complex matters Christians and scientists have one thing in common — *faith.* One of the world's greatest physicists, Nobel Prize winner Arthur H. Compton, once wrote, "Every great discovery I ever made, I gambled that the truth was there, and then I acted on it in faith until I could prove its existence."

No man adequately can imagine time before its beginning or an end that is eternal. If it could be said that God came into being at a point in time, then it would have to be said that He was created. Obviously, this reasoning, step by step backwards, would lead us to ridiculous and unending deliberations. *Faith* is a necessity.

Christ was with God "in the beginning." Therefore, Christ also existed before time. He was not "created." He also is eternal, which is more than forever, since "eternal" is not a time-concept. God gives us *faith* both to believe and to grow.

* * * * *

Since faith *is required for the Christian, does it follow some things should not be known?*

How are thinking and feeling related?

Is there a contradiction between science and religion? (Never answer any of the questions with just a 'yes' or 'no' without going into detail in your own mind.)

2nd Day — Darkness and Hostility

John 1:9-13

The greatest peril facing the Christian in society today is that he is always tempted to adjust Christian thought to a secular culture. Indeed, many would argue, we have already made the secular culture paramount and standard.

If this be true, then we have already surrendered the gospel of Jesus Christ to a movement of adaptation and accommodation. Practically this means that truth slithers and does not stand as a foundation rock.

Many denomination leaders show signs of wavering toward a gospel of thorough adjustment. One sign of this is the view that all moral law is relative. The Ten Commandments, for example, this reasoning would insist, are *sometimes* not applicable, depending upon the situation. Some call this "the new ethics."

Are there no evildoers, enemies, or wicked persons?

Jesus is the light of the world. Yet, as John tells us, the world did not want to know Jesus. Even His own people did not receive Him. Once, this made Jesus weep over the city of Jerusalem. Paul expressed what the psalmist had observed centuries before him that none is righteous, no, not one.

God did not create sin. He created man in freedom. Man has the freedom not to obey God and to sin. If it were not so, man would be no more than a beast or a robot. Genesis establishes this fact about God and creation and the existence of sin. God provides, out of love, the way out.

The world is a dark and hostile place without God. God wills goodness. Man, left to his own unaided devices in a materialistic and secular world empty of the saving grace of God, is doomed. Lonely and hostile is the heart without God. Filled and friendly is the heart with God's light.

* * * * *

In what ways has the church distorted sin?

Is it possible to live a Christian life without having enemies?

Why did Jesus criticize others, knowing that it would offend them?

Is man basically good or evil? (A reminder: detail your answer with "why?")

3rd Day — Life in the Breath of God

Job 12:7-15

Breathing in and out without conscious effort is the gift of a person with good health. When illness strikes, as in heart surgery, what a precious gift is the heart-lung machine, which gives the breath of life to the one undergoing such radical surgery. Whether in good health or ill, God is the source of life and the breath of all mankind. The truth is still valid that, as the writer of Genesis words it, ". . . the Lord God formed man of dust from the ground, and breathed into his nostrils the breath of life; and man became a living being (Gen. 2:7)."

The mystery of life, so the poets have said, is love. True as this may be, is it not first that the mystery of life is *life* — that man is a breathing, moving, vital soul?

The little baby, in the words of Grace MacDonald, seems

> Hardly a life at all,
> Only a something with hands and feet;
> Only a feeling that things are warm;
> Only a longing for something to eat.

But the little baby *is* a life, filled with the breath of all mankind. From the instant of life to the time of death, breath gives life. God gives that breath continuously, sustaining life and activity.

Most people do not utilize the life God has given to the best advantage. Someone reported seeing this epitaph: "Here lies John Brown. He died at thirty and was buried at sixty." Such a waste of breath!

When we are children it is to be expected that we would speak, think, and reason like children. When we mature, we ought to give up childish ways. Habits control what we are, what we do, and what we produce. However, habits can be changed only when we are used by great Biblical ideas.

* * * * *

Is it possible that the normal protective instinct all of us have may become destructive?

What is the relation between religion and health?

How may ideas affect our response to problems?

4th Day — Mighty Strokes of Power

Psalms 19:1-16

God to many, in and out of the Church, is the *great unreality.* Some reject Him or the idea of Him because to think about existence of a God appears to them to be ridiculous. Others have not thought of Him at all. Still others *fear* Him, that is, they are afraid of God.

In any case God is unreal. It is not easy to be neutral on the subject of the existence of God. Therefore, so great is the question one might readily speak of strong or great unbelief. Even those who are afraid of God fear Him greatly.

Many have an unreal or erroneous view of the God of the Holy Scriptures. What *is* true? He is powerful, but gentle. He is beyond finding out, yet He leaves traces of Himself everywhere. With mighty strokes He hews out valleys, rivers, and oceans. He creates. He reveals, and He makes demands of His creatures.

Why is God unreal? One suggestion that has been made is worthy of consideration. Will Herberg has criticized American religious life in his book, *Protestant-Catholic-Jew,* as being naively man-centered, sometimes expressed as faith in self, or as simply faith in faith with no object of faith indicated.

Herberg writes, "What should reach down to the core of existence, shattering and renewing, merely skims the surface of life, and yet succeeds in generating the sincere feeling of being religious."

This may be what Paul was criticizing in the Corinthians when he told them that, ". . . your faith might not rest in the wisdom of men but in the power of God (I Cor. 2:5)."

Paul always sought for the power of God in believers. He told them, "For the Kingdom of God does not consist in talk but in power (I Cor. 4:20)." In this power one will find reality.

* * * * *

What are ways you can come to know God's power without being afraid of Him?

Why did Paul object to the "words" of the Corinthians?

Why is God so unreal to many people. Is He unreal to you?

5th Day — The World Is Yours?

Genesis 1:26-31

For one week in a western city a church bulletin board proclaimed next week's sermon. The title was, "The World Is Yours." At first the title was a reminder of the Genesis account. God placed man on the earth and gave man, with His blessing, ". . . dominion over the fish of the sea and over the birds of the air and over every living thing that moves upon the earth (Gen. 1:28)."

Yet, is this account the same as saying to all who passed by, "The World is Yours?"

Does not the 24th Psalm contradict the view that the world is yours? The psalmist writes, "The earth is the Lord's and the fullness thereof, the world and those who dwell therein."

All of scripture is relevant and practical to thought and actions for today. Perhaps here this may be seen more clearly than elsewhere, and it may prompt you to search more diligently for other examples. *It matters what one thinks.*

First, there is no contradiction between the Genesis story's giving of man dominion over the earth and the 24th Psalm. As with so many other passages of the Bible, the total revelation of God must be considered and not one verse to the narrow exclusion of the whole.

Second, if someone keeps telling you that the world is yours (which is what the world is telling you all the time), you are liable eventually to believe it. The world is yours. It is up to you to take it. Take the world and all that dwells therein, its goods, its people, and use them. Use them. The world is yours.

Third, recognize the full truth. The world is God's. You and I are stewards to whom it has been given the privilege to share in God's creation. Take the goods and the people in the world to serve them. Do not use people. Serve them. They and you and the world are God's.

* * * * *

How would recognition of proper stewardship by Christians change the world?

What today reveals the fact that this is God's world, not man's?

What would your response be to the person who would tell you, "Take all you can get?"

6th Day — The Steadfast Glory

Psalms 24

Jesus healed people. He worked miracles. He astonished them, Mark writes, and the people said about Jesus, " 'He has done all things well; he even makes the deaf hear, and the dumb speak.' (Mark 7:37)."

Healing is not always physical healing. We should be amazed at what God through Jesus Christ does by sustaining people to give meaning to their lives. The steadfast glory of God!

Jesus Himself did not place the emphasis on physical healings that the people in His day and we often do. We forget that Jesus did say that we would work greater miracles than he did.

Jesus placed His emphasis in His ministry to establish the fact that the world was God's. The Father ruled, whether men acknowledged it or not.

In George Bernard Shaw's *Saint Joan,* Charles, Dauphin of France urges Joan of Arc, "Work a miracle . . . can you turn silver into gold?"

Many people want to see a miracle in order to believe. They hope by this to see God's glory. The steadfast glory of God is recognized first by acknowledging that this is God's world and that it is good. Then great miracles will come about.

Everyone has experienced a vacuum of thought and action, most when something needs to be done. You wait for the right time, the right tools, a mood, or an inspiration. Something, you say, has to come over you, and then you will know exactly what to do. With what result?

The time never comes. One month, then a year, then five and ten go by. Nothing comes over you. Nothing has been done.

Now faith sees the glory of God, the Lord strong and mighty. Such faith becomes faith-action, quite a different thing than just sitting and thinking. It is futile to wait for perfection to act. We all live by faith. Then act!

* * * * *

How did Jesus deal with questioners?

Who is the King of Glory and what does the Psalmist mean when he says He will come in?

What is the relationship of faith to probability?

7th Day — The Divine Architect

Psalms 104:1-9

Men have always tried to *prove* the existence of God to unbelievers. Eighteenth century deism took many forms. The men of that period, seeing the universe through the eyes of Galileo and Newton, thought of it as a smooth-running and beautiful machine.

But there were objections to the idea of God interfering with this universe through miracles of caring for His children. Prayer, because it seemed selfish and an attempt at man's interfering with God, was rejected.

Therefore those who wished still to believe in God without any of the "nonsense" of Biblical thought became deists. They conceived of the universe as a perfectly running clock. God, in this view, was the perfect clock maker. It would make God seem ridiculous and foolish, once the world had been created, to keep tinkering with the finished product.

Such thinking affected men in the eighteenth century in such a way, English clergy among them, that it has been said they politely bowed God out of the universe. They believed in God. However, they thought of Him as the Great Architect, the Supreme Being, or the Ancient of Days.

Dr. Geddes MacGregor has written that such a remote Deity created a religious influence through the clergy ". . . so chilly that an innkeeper is said to have observed that if he served food as cold as Parson served religion he would soon have no customers."

Yet, while one might be critical of the end result of the Deists, it must be recognized that Biblical thought often suggests that God is the Divine Architect. So He is! He laid out the world. He supervized its construction. Yet there is in Biblical thought much, much more. It is this "more" which is given to us to find out.

* * * * *

Is it possible that man can "prove" the existence of God? Does this "proof" then change the minds of others?

What are the dangers of describing God only in anthropomorphic *terms? (When you are not sure of words, use your dictionary to look up the meaning.)*

There are Biblical Christians so narrow that they cannot see the Bible as a whole. Some reject much of the Old Testament (some all of it), but believe in the New Testament. Others accept the part of the Old Testament they like such as the Genesis account.

Some of the key issues treating this problem have been presented this past week, but they have in no sense treated all the issues.

The responsible Bible student will come to know the Holy Scriptures, but will not neglect other thought or be afraid of secular ideas.

JOB 38

4 "Where were you when I laid the foun-
     dation of the earth?
  Tell me, if you have understanding.
5 Who determined its measurements—
     surely you know!
  Or who stretched the line upon it?
6 On what were its bases sunk,
     or who laid its cornerstone,
7 when the morning stars sang together,
     and all the sons of God shouted for
     joy?

THE SECOND WEEK
CREATION: BETWEEN DARKNESS AND LIGHT

Introductory Bible reading for this week:
Jeremiah 32:16-25

One might say that the writer of Proverbs presented a basic concept for the spiritual life when he wrote, "The fear of the Lord is the beginning of knowledge (1:7)." To *fear* God means to stand in awe of Him, not to be *afraid* of Him.

We may stand in awe of God because His creation seems wonderful, even beyond understanding. Therefore, we may be wise, or wisdom may begin.

However important such a basic concept might be, unless we keep alive to God's constant activity and creativity in our lives, there may be a deterioration to a common concept. Common then comes to be regarded as understood, then neglected, then misunderstood, and finally forgotten. *Fear* God the Creator, the beginning of knowledge.

1st Day — From Everlasting He Is God

Hebrews 1:1-4

Most people who refuse to ask questions about the Christian religion define *faith* as the little boy did. He said, "Faith is believing in something you know ain't so."

Logic, for example, tells us that if Jesus Christ was born in Bethlehem in Judea in a certain year and if the prophets of the Old Testament lived before that time, then Jesus could not have been God in His creation.

Jesus Himself says about Himself, "Before Abraham was, I am (John 8:58)." Not only does this appear to be illogical, but it also seems to break a few common rules of grammar. No man can speak of himself in the present tense after stating that someone in the past existed *after* him. If this approach to Jesus' pre-existence is confusing, one ought not be surprised.

It is one of the mysteries of our faith. A mystery by its very nature defies reason and logic. More importantly, for two thousand years the Church has insisted on the continuing reaffirmation of the Holy Scriptures about Christ, that is, He is both God and man. As God, Christ was in the beginning.

Language here must be used carefully, for we are not just speaking poetically. Words, admittedly, are weak vehicles to express profound truths, but they are all we have. We recognize what was once expressed by the 17th century mathematician and theologian, Blaise Pascal, as the element of risk in the life of faith and spoke of the fact that "the heart has its reasons which 'reason' does not know."

We ought not fear the asking of questions. We should be willing to look steadfastly at the deep issues of faith, the Christian faith. It is not that we shall parrot the past but rather express what *we know* of the Living God.

* * * * *

What are the different ways something may be known?

Are intellectual questions stumbling blocks to genuine faith?

Do you believe you grew up into some answers that were puzzling to you when younger? How?

2nd Day — None Can Compare

Isaiah 40:12-14

If God were fully known, he would not be God. Only creatures can be known, not the One who is before anything was, the Creator. None can compare with God or be compared to God. He stands alone. We speak about Him as being all-powerful, almighty, omniscient, and incomprehensible.

Yet, though He stands alone, He does not stand off from the world and from people. It is difficult to hold the tension of God standing *above* His creation and at the same time *with* us.

Louis I. Newman once expressed it in this way:

> *I sought to hear the voice of God,*
> *And climbed the topmost steeple,*
> *But God declared: "Go down again,*
> *I dwell among the people."*

This interpretation of the God of Abraham, Issaac, and Jacob is acceptable only in the very broadest sense. God does not sit on a cloud contemplating only that which is perfect, as the Greek philosophers thought, and since only He was perfect He contemplated only Himself.

Our God is a loving God for all His power and glory and majesty. Through His Holy Spirit, He is constantly before us wherever we may go to teach, to guide, and to help us be holy.

What we can become He directs. We have no power through our own will, and we cannot in any way merit our salvation. Grace is a gift. The power to will what we would will is a gift. Paul says he can will what is right but cannot do it. His experience is universal.

God has given man a free will. Why then does he not let it remain free? Why does he make it his own will? Only God can free man.

* * * * *

With whom or what could we try to compare to God?

Where is heaven? Is heaven really "out there?"

Do you believe most people believe in God because He really exists or because He is imagined?

3rd Day — This Great Gift

Job 38:1-11

A chamelion is any group of lizards remarkable for the changes of color of the skin according to the mood of the animal or surrounding conditions.

Man, in terms of recognition of the source of Creation and of life, is chamelion-like. Man becomes fickle and inconsistent, merging into what surrounds him. This is only another way of saying that man usually follows the crowd.

If the crowd says, "Let us make a golden calf to worship," man goes along with the suggestion. Aaron did so in the wilderness and gave one of the lamest excuses in all history when Moses questioned him about making a golden calf.

Aaron answered Moses that he took the gold and cast it into the fire, ". . . and there came out this calf (Exodus 32:24)."

Can you blame the Lord for sarcasm when He spoke to Job out of the whirlwind? "Where were you when I laid the foundation of the earth? Tell me if you have understanding. Who determined its measurements — surely you know (Job 38:4-5)?"

Many give the praise and the glory for Creation to passing fads of views which place man first and God nowhere in the scheme of things. Certainly such chamelion-like approaches must be severely criticized.

There is a famine in the land, even in the churches, of hearing the Word of the Lord. If the Word is heard and understood properly, it plows under man's pride only to raise him up a new man. What a wonderful gift of salvation!

None can avoid personal responsibility for his actions. Each person must bear his own load. Each one must face God. No one can hide in a group, taking on the coloring or the views of others. Each one must come to know personally the blunt faith-knowledge of Jesus Christ.

* * * * *

What makes you want to agree with others?
Is it possible to grow in grace without the fellowship of other believers?
Just how individual in thought and action should the Christian be?
What would life be like without God?

26

4th Day — Man Without God

Isaiah 40:27-31

A fundamental Christian position has been under attack for many decades. The attack has sometimes been successful in our society because Christians all too often have supported the adversaries.

The attack takes the form that human nature is fundamentally good and capable of progressive improvement, man is *not* prone to evil, morality and the concepts of right and wrong are psychological distortions.

When the prophet Isaiah states that the Lord gives power to the faint and shall renew the strength of the weary, must we not assume that the Lord's help is needed?

A prominent psychologist stated in a lecture that the concept of right and wrong is a distortion. He said, "For many generations we have bowed our necks to the yoke of the conviction of sin."

This sums up very well the opposition to the Biblical point of view as expressed by Paul to the Romans: "I have already charged that all men, both Jews and Greeks, are under the power of sin. . . None is righteous, no, not one (Rom. 3:9-10)."

Is this Christian position now outmoded, old-fashioned, and a relic of thought from the past? Someone has written recently that, "Within the context of industry, Christianity as it has been traditionally understood seems meaningless and God is dead."

Interestingly, present facts prove the Christian position. There is evidence that rejection of Christian thought is responsible for the upheavals of our day.

It is not degrading to admit our sinfulness. When we do see ourselves for what we are, blessed relief comes to us. We allow God to rule, as He does anyway, only now we admit it.

* * * * *

How new is the frame of thinking which suggests that man should throw off morality?

Is the mind and will of man capable of grappling with the forces of evil without divine aid?

What strength do you find in your own will?

5th Day — The Magnitude of Starry Spheres

Psalms 33:1-9

The prophet Hosea wrote of an experience he knew was valid for him and for all people when he wrote about the Lord, ". . . His going forth is as sure as the dawn; He will come to us as the showers, as the spring rains that water the earth (Hosea 6:3)."

"In the beginning God," has been the observation of men and women of all generations. More than that, He continued to sustain, strengthen and provide. He made men bold, as the prophets were in the midst of opposition.

Peter and John, brought before the Sanhedrin, spoke with strength: "For we cannot but speak of what we have seen and heard (Acts 4:20)."

They were people of faith looking to God for their salvation, seeing Him everywhere to such an extent they were able to endure to the end. Of them the writer of Hebrews observed: "Quenched raging fire, escaped the edge of the sword, won strength out of weakness, became mighty in war, put foreign armies to flight (11:34)."

All of them, just as we are, were able to look into the magnitude of the starry spheres, into themselves to discover that His strength and grace made weakness as nothing.

Such people are the people of God, not some lunatics believing in fiction and fables. From God came vital impulses and revelations. They knew as the remnant of believers know today that the sovereignty of God is at stake. He is the central sun round which everything in life revolves and evolves.

He is God the supreme and absolute ruler in creation, in providence, and in redemption.

No wonder then the Psalmist could say, "For he spoke, and it came to be commanded, and it stood forth (Psalms 33:9)."

* * * * *

How would you respond to the words of a university student, "There is no absolute truth"?

Has knowledge of our world and the universe grown to the degree where we can dispense with God?

Do we live in an orderly world?

6th Day — Fields Wet With Diamond Dew

Psalms 65:9-13

The first time anyone sees the Grand Canyon he can hardly believe his eyes: the steep cliffs, the ribbon-like river, and the great splashes of changing colors.

Old Faithful, at Yellowstone Park, is only one of many geysers in the park. There are a myriad of pools which bubble gases out of the bowels of the earth. The deep Norwegian fjords are breathtaking.

Man's marvels affect us in similar ways: great dams and bridges, tunnels and aqueducts, subways and skyscrapers. Yet, what man creates is still only a *copy* of the wonders created by God. The river of God is filled with water, as the psalmist observes.

The world and God's bounty are good. When we become aware, truly awakened, our small and narrow world suddenly enlarges, and it becomes a world of wonder and awe, a world of rich moods and shadows, a great and fascinating world.

Yet God's bounty to us only begins with that which can be seen. He gives us also the unseen world, especially when snares, distresses, and the cords of death would strangle us. Then God in His love gives us His deliverance and becomes our Savior. He reaches from on high, according to the 18th Psalm, he takes us, draws us out of the deep waters.

We are often so foolish when it comes to God. Casualness characterizes our understanding. Oh yes, He created the heavens and the earth. He gives us food, shelter, home, and family. It is only as we see the fullness of His bounty, in the unseen but nevertheless real world of ourselves in our human needs, shortcomings, and weaknesses, that we come fully to know Him.

Let us come to know Him through the seen world. But let us also know Him in the unseen world and as our Savior.

* * * * *

What is religion: a book, an organization, or a set of rules and regulations? Have you allowed God to show you the wonders of the unseen world? How would you describe the unseen world?

7th Day — How Unsearchable Is God?

Psalms 24:1-6

"Can we see God?" is the question of a child. "No," we must answer, "here we cannot see God."

There are times even when we despair for our very souls. We reach a canyon wall which cannot be scaled. The turbulence of human emotion becomes like a raging river. Despair comes at every turn, every idea, and every attitude which helped us so in the past. What can we do?

The only answer is, "Worship the Creator."

Think, read, explain, consider — but above all things, worship. Worship may be corporate and private praise and prayer. It may be varied from elaborate and complicated ritual to the ejaculations of spontaneous private devotion. Worship in church ought not be a concert to be listened to but rather an activity in which one is participating.

Rudyard Kipling once summed up the attitude of the worshipper and his need as follows:

> The tumult and the shouting dies,
> The captains and the kings depart;
> Still stands the ancient sacrifice,
> An humble and a contrite heart.
> Lord God of hosts, be with us yet,
> Lest we forget, lest we forget.

There is always the problem of creating a substitute for God so that what is worshipped is in God's place. Jesus said that we cannot worship God and riches. We cannot divide ourselves into deceitful ways without suffering the consequences. Our devotion must be singleminded.

If we genuinely believe in God, that He is the Creator and to Him belong glory, honor, and praise, we will not let any person or thing take His place. Follow the advice given in *Revelation*.

John had received so many revelations he was moved to fall down at the feet of an angel to worship him. The angel warned John: "Worship God (Rev. 22:9)."

* * * * *

Do you worship God daily?

Why do you believe Jesus used our *instead of* my *in teaching his followers the Lord's prayer?*

How is the learning process related to worship?

30

You should be concerned more about the things you do understand in the Holy Scriptures than the things you do not understand. If you understand the words, "In the beginning God," then live by them. You will then come to know the meaning of the resurrection and the words, "He is risen!"

The relationship between the Old and New Testaments will become clearer. God has a plan for you, your family, and His Church.

Submit your will daily to read, with an open mind and free will, the words of life.

PROVERBS 27

1 Do not boast about tomorrow,
for you do not know what a day
may bring forth.

THE THIRD WEEK
THE LAMP OF THE LORD

**Introductory Bible reading for this week:
Psalms 8**

In society the old foundations have been slipping and crumbling for many years. One, belief in God. Two, everything that happens in the world has a purpose. Three, there is a world moral order. Four, God created man for a purpose.

As a Christian you have a double responsibility. You cannot turn your back on the fact that the changes are taking place. At the same time, you must be willing to reexamine your own faith periodically.

God created man in his own image, true, but what is meant by "the image of God (Gen. 1:27)?" An image is a reflection. It is not a physical image. The writer of Proverbs gives us an excellent picture here when he writes, "The spirit of man is the lamp of the Lord (Prov. 20:27)." You are the Lord's lamp.

1st Day — Beyond Excellence

Psalms 8

We know that the old order changes and makes way for the new. However, today a *plus* has been added. Scientific and technological developments, psychological insights, and the rise of new world views all have thrust each of us into a completely new frame of reference.

What has happened is revolutionary and radical in its impact. There are many who would regard the words of the psalmist as only poetry, without significant meaning: "O Lord, our Lord, how majestic is they name in all the earth (Ps. 8:9)!"

His name is majestic! Of course. Beyond majestic! Beyond excellence! This is poetry with tremendous meaning. Religious language is varied. Truth is expressed in many ways.

An old English litany contains this petition: "Good Lord, deliver us from goblins and beasties and from things that go *whoosh* in the night."

Our language might be slightly different but we have our own goblins and beasties: apprehensions, fears, dread, meaninglessness, and anxiety. Daily all of us face a dilemma.

A natural response might be to take hold of God, or try to, to have Him do our bidding, instead of asking Him to take hold of us so we do His will. It is in the spirit of man the answer is found.

The lamp of the Lord! He has created us in *His* image, and we become His Light. We are not *the* light. We are a reflection of the light of the world, Christ, the true Light, which lighteth every man that cometh into the world (John 1:9).

Just as John the Baptist was not that Light (John 1:8) so we are not that Light, but like John we are sent to bear witness of that Light. The lamp of the Lord.

The world would destroy all this for you and me, just as in Jesus' day. Therefore the changes of the day while new for us are like faith-problems of old.

* * * * *

Explain what is meant by a scientific view of the world. How does it differ from the Biblical?

What is the main purpose of man's creation?

How would you explain that God is the same yesterday and forever?

2nd Day — Our Arm Every Morning

Matthew 12:9-13

There seems to be a contradiction between the values of a man and the sickness of which Jesus speaks. The whole need not a physician but they that are sick (Matthew 9:12).

Jesus does not question the value of a man. He also acknowledges that God is strength, in fact being our arm every morning (Is. 33:2). Further, the world and all God created is good (Gen. 1:31).

Jesus does heal the sick, but the sickness of which Jesus speaks so frequently is the sickness of the soul and the need for justification. No man is saved by works, but justification comes by faith (Rom. 1:17). Although the old moorings in our day are slipping, the problems have not basically changed.

The thoughts and actions of all of us tend to be governed or at the least influenced by some set of general ideas about the nature of the world and man's place in it. This may be called a world-picture, or as the Germans say, *Weltanschauung,* a favorite word of theologians and philosophers.

In the majority of men this world-picture works unseen, a dim background in their minds, unnoticed by themselves because taken for granted. Christians ought be aware of this subtle influence and take steps to understand and, when necessary, to combat it. You would not want to be caught unaware. You could be.

The reason is that this world-picture, which every generation of man has had, normally changes so slowly that men can adjust to the changes and retain what is valuable in the old and see it in relation to the new and adjust to it.

You and I, however, have inherited a recolutionary world-picture. We have to admit that the world and values have changed radically. There is upheaval everywhere. This does not change but rather accentuates our need to remain close to God by daily reading and thought about His word.

* * * * *

What are some of the things which have changed in your lifetime in the world?

Explain how the changes might or might not be considered good or bad?

In daily life, apart from prayer and reading the Scriptures, what else could you do for guidance?

3rd Day — Living, Moving, Being

Acts 17:24-28

The great missionary, Paul, once spoke to the Athenians on Mars Hill. Their frame of mind was telling or hearing something new (Acts 17:21). One could certainly liken them to people in our day who have no interest in past values.

Professor Stace in *Religion and the Modern Mind* describes what is new in our time, in terms of the world-picture which has developed through science for our day. Let us make it very clear that *some* think this way quite seriously now, but we cannot deny that it seems gradually moving toward being the dominant view of our times. There are three aspects.

First, the world is wholly governed by blind physical forces. Second, the world is entirely senseless and meaningless. Third, the whole universe is indifferent to values of any kind. All morality is subjective and relative.

Paul challenges the Athenians, as well we might today, that God made everything that is (Acts 17:25) and that in God we live, and move, and have our being (Acts 17:28). Paul's thought is quite philosophical here, and there is a place for such responses.

Jesus is just as profound, though he states his views more simply, when he tells his followers that God knows of our needs and provides for them (Mt. 6:32). When you try to reason out the subtle thinking of scientists and philosophers today, follow also Jesus' advice. He tells his followers he sends them out into the world as sheep in the midst of wolves, ". . . so be wise as serpents and innocent as doves (Mt. 10:16)."

In that connection, recognize as you face what the world is saying through scientific discoveries that are called *modern*, not all that is said is sound.

There is no official scientific view. Scientific observations do not automatically lead to the conclusions described by Professor Stace. Be wise as a serpent in recognizing these facts. Stand your ground.

* * * * *

What are the values in reading about views which may appear to contradict Christian thought?

Why is "simple trust" not quite the same thing as having an ignorant mind?

Describe in detail your world-picture. Write it out.

4th Day — Everyone Is A Servant

Philippians 2:5-11

The scientific view described earlier can and does for many people destroy Christian faith, but it does not have to do so. God is both above and in the world. He is in science and the scientists. This field and the men in it could not exist but for God.

God rules science and scientists just as he does the whole world and every other man-centered endeavor.

However, a great many people are influenced by these views, often unknowingly. We are influenced, no matter how strong we think our faith is. Of course we can become intelligent and learn how to argue logically and rationally. Why should we not become wise as serpents? It is not a contradiction to the Christian way.

That is one way. Another way equally stressed by Christ is to be innocent as doves (Mt. 10:16).

Within the context of the entire text, or for that matter all Christian thought, reason is upheld and has a high place. The difference between the Christian and those of the world is that the Christian takes one more step. Some regard this step as irrational. He becomes a servant of others.

Jesus Christ is his example. How firm a foundation is Jesus Christ our Lord, might well be our desire and aim this day and always. The foundations of the world and the thought world in which we live have not really slipped. We are the ones who either have or are in danger of slipping.

Christ emptied Himself of his divinity and took on the form of a servant (Phil. 2:6-7), and we should have the same mind (2:5) because we too are to be servants. Consider this. Begin slowly, but begin.

Each day is a new beginning. We need not wait until tomorrow. As suggested by James Russell Lowell:

> Greatly begin! though thou have time
> But for a line, be that sublime —
> Not failure, but low aim is crime.

* * * * *

If we are saved by faith and not works, why nevertheless should works follow faith?

In the light of the theme that everyone is a servant, how can you be a lamp of the Lord?

How would you explain the words "innocent as a dove" to a little child?

5th Day — Look to Jesus

Hebrews 2:5-9

If Jesus is a servant and if we are all to become servants, then it follows that God's plan is found in Jesus Christ. We ought then look to Jesus as a pattern and a guide.

There is a purpose for this, for we have a task to do and many responsibilities. God did not give angels the same responsibility as to us, and He rather put the world in subjection under the feet of man (Heb. 1:5,8)).

Later in Hebrews this theme is developed more fully. Examples of faithful men and women are given in the 11th chapter of Hebrews. Immediately thereafter, the Christian is challenged by these examples as follows:

"Therefore, since we are surrounded by so great a cloud of witnesses, let us also lay aside every weight, and sin which clings so closely, and let us run with perserverance the race that is set before us, looking to Jesus, the pioneer and perfecter of our faith (Heb. 12:1-2)."

These witnesses acted by faith, even when their world was breaking up. Some when they were young, like Abel and Moses, gave of their gifts to God. Abel died early. Moses saved a people by going into a wilderness for forty years to train them for the better life they were going to have.

Some were old, like Abraham, and went out from their settled life to a life of promise. He did not know the final outcome. Yet Abraham became the father of a nation. Age is no deterrent to changing and improving the world. They were all pilgrims.

Many, many years ago someone loved you a great deal to bring you to where you are. Gifts were given, not earned. They were pilgrims. So are you.

Pilgrims always build pilgrims. We were loved. We love. We were given. We give. We create pilgrims of the future. Look to Jesus' example.

* * * * *

Explain how you and other Christians may be pioneers and pilgrims without leaving home.

What examples, both good and bad, have had influences on your life?

What special values come to all of us when we share our faith with others?

6th Day — Never Underestimate God

Psalms 103:1-5

All of us need to recognize that we do not need to carry the problems of the world all by ourselves. The fact is that we do not, no matter what we think is our strength or importance.

Honesty forces us to state, "Bless the Lord, O my soul, and forget not all his benefits (Ps. 103:2)." We march by promise because someone before us marched by promise. We do not do it alone. All people march by promise, even unbelievers. The promise is the promise of God. We should never underestimate God. He does for us all far better things than we know or can pray for or imagine.

Life is often a series of burdens. The world ignores our dreams and hopes. It shapes itself for us into distortions of what it could be — the burden of frustration.

We often are wasted and weakened by illness, and age gradually takes its toll — the burden of physical weakness.

Or, we often feel the pressures of conflict and distress — the burden of hopelessness.

Sin also clings so closely. The spirit tires and the mind and flesh wander into a world of lawlessness of desires and longings. Subtly we tend to steal the things and the character of others. We try to buy and coerce the shape of the world to match our own image of it.

Never underestimate the power of God, for He has given us Jesus the author and finisher of our faith. (Heb. 12:2). No wonder the psalmist can say that God forgives all our iniquities, heals our diseases, redeems us from destruction, and who crowns each of us with loving-kindness and tender mercies! Jesus is proof of it.

To look to Jesus is to look to God. The cloud of witnesses, parents and grandparents and many before them, were pilgrims only because they looked to God.

So we can lay aside every burden and look also to God. This week do it in church and in the Scriptures.

* * * * *

What are the ways you have underestimated the power and action of God in your life?

What are the ways you can improve so as not to continue to make these mistakes?

Describe the values of fellowship in worship.

7th Day — Kindness In His Mercy

Psalms 103:15-22

Some Christians have suggested abandoning the Trinitarian formula of Father, Son, and Holy Spirit. The Trinity may be a great mystery, but it is needed because it expresses a great truth.

Jesus Christ is the personification of the Creator-Sanctifier. What is needed is not abandonment but a deeper and more personal grasping of how God reveals Himself to men.

Jesus was true man. He lived in times like ours. His nation was a captive nation. Even in His day the religious leaders of His nation thwarted the purposes of God. They twisted God's message into their message. The message of men!

Fortunately for men God does not deal with us on the basis of our sins and iniquities (Ps. 103:10). He is merciful. There is kindness in His mercy. It is from everlasting to everlasting (Ps. 103:17).

Jesus is from everlasting to everlasting. He is very God of very God. Jesus pioneered and perfected our faith. He shook every weight. He rejected sin, though he was tempted (Heb. 2:18). He died for us, God showing his love for us (Rom. 5:8).

No wonder we can say then with the psalmist, "Bless the Lord (Ps. 103:21)."

The psalmist is filled with revelations constantly of mercy and, especially hope. "And hope does not disappoint us, because God's love has been poured into our hearts through the Holy Spirit which has been given to us (Rom. 5:5)."

Neglect Father, Son, and Holy Spirit in our praise, and we will have rejected God. Listen to the so-called wise theologians of our day who would destroy the Trinity, and we will have strangled Christian faith.

As Martin Luther has written about the Trinity, you must ". . . listen only to what God says of Himself, and of His innermost being. In no other way can we know this. And there God's folly and the world's wisdom clash."

Let it clash! A proper battle for so good a Lord!

* * * * *

What are the gifts given to each of us without deserving them?
How do you explain that they are the gifts of God?
If the Trinity is a mystery, what are the ways God opens up understanding of Himself?

If you are in darkness because there is no electricity, consider how welcome a member of your family or a friend is who carries a lamp, or flashlight, and brings light into darkness.

Take it one step farther. Suppose you are carrying the lamp for a member of your family or a friend. The light you carry would be most welcome.

God gives each of us the privilege to be His candle in this world. You are worth a great deal not only to Him but to others for whom by your spirit and reflection of the "image of God" you light the way to Christ. Let your light shine.

PSALM 71

Thou who hast done great things,
   O God, who is like thee?
20 Thou who hast made me see many sore
     troubles
   wilt revive me again;
from the depths of the earth
   thou wilt bring me up again.
21 Thou wilt increase my honor,
   and comfort me again.

THE FOURTH WEEK
BEING GOOD IS NOT ENOUGH

Introductory Bible reading for this week:
Romans 3:9-22a

Those who seriously attempt to read and understand Paul's letters, especially *Romans,* probably will be struck with two impresssions. The first is one of clear and great flashes of insight in the thought of the great missionary. The second is the difficulty of Pauline thought when he explains important points of theology.

On the other hand, Jesus' thought and meaning are usually quite clear. A parable illustrates a specific teaching. Occasionally, however, Jesus utters a statement which creates a problem, as when he said, "You, therefore, must be perfect, even as your heavenly Father is perfect (Mt. 5:48)."

Jesus says, "Be perfect." Or, be good. The problem of sin is at the heart of Jesus' teaching.

1st Day — Forgive Them Not?

Romans 1:18-23

When the apostle Paul creates a theological problem, the believer is most likely to ask, "What does Paul mean?" The search takes the form of digging for the answer.

When Jesus' ideas create a problem, the believer sometimes wants to ask, "Is this what Jesus really means?" Some might go so far as to say about some of Jesus' teachings, "Surely Jesus does not mean this except in an allegorical sense."

The purpose in suggesting this contrast between Jesus and Paul is neither to point out that Jesus is the better teacher — which he is — nor is it to suggest that Paul was at odds with Jesus — which he was not.

The purpose is to counteract the error of explaining away all of Jesus' sayings by the reasoning that the Gospels reveal only the mind of the early church.

In other words, only the early church, not Jesus, is reflected in the teaching of the Gospels. To expand this, some say that the writers of the Gospels put only their ideas of the developing Christian community into the Gospels and made Jesus parrot these ideas. In other words, they were willing to twist our Lord's views to suit their own bias and for purposes of Christian propaganda.

If these thoughts are offensive to you, they should be. But it should not blind you to the fact that many strong churches have clergy trained in this way of thinking. Trained, in other words, (1) *to explain away both the historical and the divine Jesus and (2) to destroy the heart of the Gospel of Jesus' teaching: man is in need of saving because he is sinful.*

Biblical criticism is a necessary and valuable discipline to guide the Bible student. This should not be forgotten. "Blind" study serves the sincere student poorly. However, a warped approach to the Gospel has always been a threat to Biblical teaching. Such Christian leaders would explain sin away, or say sin does not exist. They would caricature the "wrath of God (Rom. 1:18)" and say God could not be that wicked.

If God were that wicked it would mean that His theme would really be "Forgive Them Not," not a message of forgiveness and justification through belief (Rom. 4:3-5). God does pass judgment on sin, but God loves and saves (John 3:16-17) the sinner.

* * * * *

What does Jesus mean by the teaching, "You, therefore, must be perfect, as your heavenly Father is perfect?"

What purpose would any church leader have who deemphasizes the sinful nature of man?

Whose teaching is in the Gospels? Why?

44

2nd Day — Terror of the Lord

Romans 2:1-5

Jonathan Edwards' sermon dealing with sinners in the hands of an angry God, as part of the religious life of the 18th century, deserves to be the landmark it has become in American religious history.

"A most terrible sermon," one listener wrote, "which should have had a word of Gospel at the end of it, though I think 'tis all true." Jonathan Edwards did preach the full Gospel. His reputation in its negative aspects is not deserved, although he frightened thoroughly all who heard him regarding the terror of the Lord.

Edwards understood the wrath and terror of the Lord, and he preached eloquently about it. But he should be more well known than he is for his *Treatise Concerning Religious Affections,* which he completed in 1746.

He was not advocating a return to emotionalism, as one historian analyzes the treatise, but Edwards was attempting to prove that religion is not primarily an affair of the intellect, but an affair of the heart.

As Edwards himself states it, "True religion consists very much in affections." Or, in another place, "If the great things of religion are rightly understood, they will affect the heart."

It was a stress for inner witness, not just of the mind, but of the emotions. In the breadth of his insight, Jonathan Edwards walked in the same pathway as Paul, Augustine, Luther, and Wesley.

The terror of the Lord, a valid sense of punishment and wrath, can only be understood fully by those who know that the degree of God's love is immeasurable. "O the depth of the riches and wisdom and knowledge of God!" Paul cried out to the Romans (11:33).

You, Jesus says, be perfect. For your growth in grace, know God's wrath *and* love.

*   *   *   *   *

How might it be possible that stress on the love of God would lead only to lukewarm Christians?

Have you ever benefited by punishment (wrath) from any source? How? Describe it to someone.

Start to keep a written record of sermon themes.

3rd Day — The Law and Judgment

Romans 2:12-16

Paul carefully details how God's judgment is visited upon both the Jew and the Gentile. That judgment is to "render to every man according to his works (Rom. 2:6)." This rule of judgment holds universally. "For God shows no partiality (Rom. 2:11)."

In the day of God's judgment God will judge the secrets of men by Jesus Christ (Rom. 2:16).

The law, therefore, and judgment according to it, is a law which the Gospel of grace has not changed. Consider it in the light of previous thought about Jesus stating that we must be perfect, as our heavenly Father is perfect.

Concerning the reliability of the Gospels in reporting what Jesus said accurately there can be no doubt whatsoever.

The difficulty of the saying for modern man lies in his unwillingness to believe in a religion which breaks his pride, one that challenges his definition of religion as simply living the good life or being good.

Being good is not enough. Putting on the outward trappings of the pious is not enough. A religion of rules, doing certain *religious things* and avoiding certain *non-religious things,* is not enough.

Authentic Christianity is meaningless except as a religion of salvation for those of broken pride. It is for sinners and not for the self-righteous.

From its beginnings until now, Christianity's first task has always been that of smashing man's self-trust and turning him into a seeker of salvation outside himself. *Its first gift is the gift of a bad conscience.*

No wonder, then, that men have always wanted to explain away Jesus' clear utterances as exaggerations!

Sit quietly each morning, reflect on all that God puts in the mind, read His Word, and pray.

* * * * *

What are the things people generally regard as being religious? Write them down.

Are they really religious?

Is it possible to make convenient compartments for the religious and non-religious in life?

If you answer, yes or no, why?

4th Day — You Are My Servants

Romans 3:1-8

God told His people, the Jews, "You are my servants." Therefore, the Jews had an advantage. Paul writes, "To begin with, the Jews are entrusted with the oracles of God (Rom. 3:2)." But they refused to be servants, except a remnant, and the responsibility was given to the Gentiles. "You," God says, "be my servants."

None can boast. None can ridicule another, for both Jew and Gentile are under judgment. Who then are left to be God's servant? Who are God's chosen ones since there is none righteous (Rom. 3:10)?

It is not only a question of willingness to follow Jesus. There must be a setting aside of one's riches (whatever counts most), *then* to follow Him (Luke 18:18:23).

It means self-surrender. Jesus' teachings mean the breaking of the illusion of man that he controls himself and the world. They mean tearing down the walls a man might erect to avoid anxiety, the tradegy of time and the times, the dread of loneliness, the burden of guilt and the defiance of the heart.

"You, therefore, must be perfect" — take it to heart. But you might say, if being good is not enough, then why strive for perfection? A contradiction is not possible.

The answer must be given: "No, it is not a contradiction. It may be a paradox, but it is not a contradiction. To strive for perfection, to be perfect as the heavenly Father is perfect, is the means whereby Jesus wishes us to see ourselves through God's eyes and to submit to God in complete self-surrender daily."

To be good in the ordinary sense of that term may be possible. It may mean being as good as or better than one's neighbor. It may mean attending church when many people do not. Goodness in these terms is always measured in terms of other people.

But compare yourself to God's perfection and love. See where you stand. Will *you* be His servant?

* * * * *

What are some of Jesus' teachings which also might be considered as not to be literally interpreted?

Having listed some of these, now ask yourself why you might divide them into those to be followed quite literally and those not? Give sound reasons.

5th Day — Everlasting Burnings

Romans 3:9-18

When Paul charges that, "No one is righteous, no, not one; no one understands, no one seeks after God (Rom. 3:10-22)," he reflects Jesus' teaching (Mk. 7:15, Lk. 11:14) and the Old Testament.

Jew and Greek are all under the power of sin (Ps. 14:1-2; 53:1-2; Is. 59:7-8). Sin and rebellion against God are universal. They are pervasive. The first man, Adam, sinned (Gen 3). God gave Adam and Eve a free will, but both refused to let it remain free. They followed their own wills. Punishment followed.

Earlier Jonathan Edwards' sermon, "Sinners in the Hands of an Angry God," was referred to as showing the anger and wrath of God. The sermon could also have been titled, "Everlasting Burnings."

It has been reported of that congregation in New England in the 18th Century, "Some of those sitting in the pews would remember this very discourse in hell. If we knew who they were . . . But at that point, he might as well have called the names. His hearers knew who they were, as they caught hold of the pillars of the building and cried out in helpless panic."

Such sermons may have gone out of style, but one thing can be said for certain: Jonathan Edwards described Biblical truth. Edwards' reputation has been based almost exclusively on this one exposition of the wrath of God. This is unkind and unfair. But he did try to preach the truth. One cannot ignore guilt of sin and the punishment which would follow.

It has been reported of one Christian body that after they had approved a strong statement about God's wrath and punishment, one member protested that it said nothing about the love of God.

Another innocently suggested, "Let us stress the love of God in a footnote to the statement."

Another thundered, "Relegate the love of God to a footnote!" Hurriedly the body revised the entire statement.

* * * * *

Steadily, daily, put some time aside to reflect on your sins and God's way out for you.

Consider this: how would systematic Bible reading help your life? Write down your answer and tell someone.

Can you have good news and keep quiet? Why not?

6th Day — Stability of Our Times

Romans 3:21-26

The stability of our times is not your or my righteousness — it is the grace-gift of the righteousness of God through faith in Jesus Christ (Rom. 3:22). It does no injustice either to proper Biblical exposition to leave off the phrase in that verse which states "for all who believe" or the entire treatment of Paul about grace in Romans.

For one thing, that verse clearly states that God gives his gifts "for all" and then adds, "For there is no distinction." Jesus often said that.

God makes his sun to rise on the evil and on the good, and sends rain on the just and on the unjust (Mt. 5:45).

The stability of our times is dependent not on our righteousness but on God's. It would seem, for example, that the Pharisee (Lk. 18:11) who boasted of his goodness was good, but this kind of goodness was not good enough.

The tax collector, on the other hand, would not even lift up his eyes to heaven, "but beat his breast, saying, 'God be merciful to me a sinner (Luke 18:13)'."

The Pharisee, quite obviously, was not fulfilling Jesus' command, "You, therefore, must be perfect, as your heavenly Father is perfect (Mt. 5:48)."

The Pharisee was not placing his goodness under the revealing light of God's perfect righteousness and love and found wanting. The tax collector did compare himself to God's perfection and love and discovered or revealed himself as a sinner.

In his apparent moment of success, the Pharisee had failed. In his apparent moment of failure, the tax collector was successful or, better, saved.

The truth is that even if both men had failed, their failure would have had no affect on the grace-gift of God's righteousness through faith in Jesus Christ. The stability of our times — and our salvation — is Almighty God, Father, Son, and Holy Spirit.

* * * * *

What are some of the obvious reasons we must compare our righteousness to God's, not our neighbor's?

Go beyond the obvious and ask, why do all of us like to avoid talk about punishment and wrath?

Why — go deep — do we love to stress love only?

7th Day — Faithful and Sure

Romans 3:27-31

Paul stresses the fact that there are no gods but only One God. He is the God of all, of the Jews and of the Gentiles, and He is One (Rom. 3:29-30).

Jonah did not want to believe that God was One, and that His concern stretched out to the people of the city of Nineveh (Jon. 1:1-2). Men do act selfishly about God as with everything else, desiring His exclusive concern for them, their families and their nation.

Jesus' Great Commission is for his followers to go into all the world, teaching and baptizing in His name (Mt. 28:19-20). This was Jesus' answer to the fact that being good was not enough.

The man who is an alcoholic may be a failure, but it may also be the means whereby he might look at himself for the first time to see what he really is, to see the sham, the insincerity, the false pride, and the wrong means he is using to answer these problems.

The couple who see their marriage shaking and showing a cracking at the seams, may be at the point of truth for the first time.

The business man whose fortune is slipping away, may discover it can become his moment of greatness.

In no sense ought one seek to be an alcoholic, or to create difficulties in one's marriage, or to strive to lose one's fortune or business to prove a point about religion or human nature. The start could be, though, what is *your* problem? What tacks are in your shoes?

Failure is proof of potential greatness. Failure may begin learning. The great wonder of the spirit and the mind of man given by God is that a man can perceive the truth and follow it *before* he needs to be humbled by tragic experiences.

The nature of the perfection toward which Jesus demands that we follow is patterned after the Holy One Himself. The righteousness which exceeds that of the scribes and Pharisees is the union of righteousness and love. Being good is not enough. The Pharisee was good, but he was cold, opinionated, and selfish.

* * * * *

In the record keeping of sermon themes which was suggested earlier, note if they speak to your needs.

If being good is not enough, how would you explain the necessity for right living?

What is the relationship between faith and works?

Any careful reading of the Holy Scriptures makes you realize that God desires our goodness and calls on us to fulfill His laws and commandments. Jesus said in the Sermon on the Mount, "Think not that I have come to abolish the law and the prophets; I have come not to abolish them but to fulfill them (Mt. 5:17)."

JAMES 3

⁵ So the tongue is a little member and boasts of great things. How great a forest is set ablaze by a small fire! 6 And the tongue is a fire.

THE FIFTH WEEK
FROZEN WORDS, HOT DEEDS

Introductory Bible reading for this week:
Matthew 5:21-26

A lawyer once objected when Jesus said, "You shall love the Lord your God ... and your neighbor as yourself (Lk. 10:27). The objection of the lawyer took the form of a question, "And who is my neighbor (Lk. 10:29)?"

The basis of the lawyer's objection was that it is precisely when one begins to put such a rule into practice that difficulties arise. Where does one draw the line between the neighbor and the non-neighbor? Who should have this consideration?

There must have been scorn in the voice of the lawyer, out of exclusiveness and pride. Hear the scorn in the voices of men and women over all the world, in you and me: "And who is my neighbor?"

Cold words! Frozen. Hate comes, then violence.

1st Day — Watchmen of the Lord

I John 3:1-3

Jesus always adds new dimensions to every Old Testament law. First, he does not deny the law and its value. He does not come to destroy the law but to fulfill it (Mt. 5:17-18).

Second, Jesus makes the law positive. Fulfilling the law leads to greatness in the kingdom of heaven (Mt. 5:19). Third, he deepens the concept of the law. Breaking the law is more than *doing the breaking*. Adultery, for example, is not only in the act but in the *looking* and the *thought* (Mt. 5:27-28). Further, breaking the command, "You shall not kill," is also expressed in anger (Mt. 5:21-25).

Fifth, Jesus expands the concept of discipleship. It is not enough *not* to break laws. The disciple should act with concern and compassion toward his neighbors. He must have their welfare at heart and seek positive ways to express this.

Cain answered the Lord, after killing his brother Abel, with a sarcastic question: "Am I my brother's keeper (Gen. 4-9)?"

Yes, the disciple of Christ is his brother's keeper. The law is laid down to love God and to love one's neighbor (Lk. 10:27). Not only are we to show concern with words, but by actions. Try loving your neighbor like yourself. *Watch* out over him. Have his interest at heart. You are a son or a daughter of God.

The world may react against us by reason of this because the world does not know His love (I John 3:1). But, watch and pray (Mk. 13:33), and also be watchmen of the Lord (Is. 21:6).

Both are required of a disciple — to watch himself and to watch or care for others. The reason should be very clear.

Sin is a powerful force, which blinds all men. Sin leads to all manner of deviations from the way of the Lord, the works of the flesh as Paul lists them in his letter to the Galatians (5:19-21). Be watchmen.

* * * * *

What are the sources of rebellion and sin against God and one's neighbor? How does God assist each of us to fight sin?

Consider ways you can be a watchman, without at the same time meddling, with your friends.

2nd Day — Darkness for Light

I John 3:4-10

Is it possible to have enemies and be a Christian? Is it conceivable that the Christian might hate wrongdoing? Should there be a distinction between the Christian and the non-Christian in society?

No doubt you would answer all these questions with a "Yes." Jesus had enemies. He hated wrongdoing without hating the wrongdoer. He pointed out in many ways the distinctions between His followers and those who were against Him.

There is lawlessness in your life, the neighborhood in which you live, in the country, and in the world. We should not be deceived about the existence of lawlessness (I Jn. 3:7). Love in itself is *not* the answer *unless* there is a recognition that darkness exists in the world in the forms of sin, rebellion, hatred, violence, and murder. None can close his eyes to the existence of this dark side of human nature.

A philosopher has been described as one who has learned the art of being unhappy intelligently.

The Christian perhaps, in the light of the opposing forces of darkness and light, should be described as one who has learned the art of being opposed to the ways of the world lovingly.

Who can deny this? An open-eyed and honest view of the world would have to recognize the enmities of hatred and love, the enemy and friend, and darkness and light.

Many Christians refuse to acknowledge these distinctions. If they do in general terms, they often fail to delineate properly between them and how to respond to them.

Note and take heed to the prayer of the psalmist: "Stretch forth thy hand from on high, rescue me and deliver me from the many waters, from the hand of aliens, whose mouth speaks lies, and whose right hand is a right hand of falsehood. (Ps. 144:7-8)."

Aliens are those opposed to the ways of God.

*   *   *   *   *

Who are your enemies? Have you caused the problem which creates enmity?

Why did Jesus speak harshly against the Pharisees and Sadducees when he knew he would offend them?

Consider, then practise a proper love to others.

3rd Day — Light for Darkness

I John 3:11-18

No darkness is ever unrelieved for God's watchmen. God gives His light to you, thus giving you power to give light to others to relieve the darkness in the world for others and for yourself.

When the psalmist asks the Lord for deliverance from aliens, it is as though he were saying, "Help me, O God, to recognize those who are not of Thee, who do not follow Thy ways. I need deliverance, Lord, because it is all too easy for me to wish to believe in others, to desire to conform to them because it is the more congenial way."

To be able to recognize the aliens is a gift of God. Such a person may even stimulate your faith because he may get you to realize that you have been living on baby food theologically. Such food is inadequate and deficient to meet the rigors of the ethical and moral demands of our day.

We should not be surprised that the world hates us (I Jn. 3:13). Do not be surprised if Christians hate you. Abel was hated by Cain. Jesus was hated by His own people. This should make us realize something extremely significant. The world, sometimes Christians, does not like light but rather darkness.

You may have an enemy because you have wronged him, but perhaps that is not the case. He may be your enemy because you stand for something that reveals his own darkness contrasted by your light.

Some Christians reason that if one has enemies it is certainly to have been caused by not being loving or kind enough. All means have not been exhausted to follow Jesus' command to love one another.

It is most necessary that we do all in our power to prevent friction. *But,* Christians are in the midst of non-Christians. Some people have unclean lips and deceitful hearts. They like darkness.

With all hypocrisy put aside, it may at times be necessary to oppose others lovingly.

* * * * *

What distinctions would you make between hatred and love for use in practical living?

Why might you not give to every person who has a need who comes along?

How are denial and opposition a form of love?

4th Day — Chirp and Mutter

James 3:1-12

From this passage from James one may get the impression that *in itself* the tongue is evil. After all, it might be argued, the tongue is called "a restless evil, full of deadly poison (James 3:8)."

The tongue is not evil in itself. It is used also for blessing God (James 3:9-10). It is at this point wise to point out that James tells the truth. Trouble is caused by wagging and vicious tongues that are left uncontrolled.

One other reminder is also necessary. Back of the tongue so inclined is an unredeemed heart and mind. All Scripture needs to be balanced by the whole of Scripture, a sound principle for the interpretation of God's Word.

Back of the tongue, in Jesus' words, is inner defilement (Mk. 7:15.) To change the tongue and its unruly activity the inner man must be changed. The inner man cannot be changed apart from faith in Jesus Christ. Then all of life will change, including the tongue.

The casual speech, the shaded speech toward partial truth, and the talking without thought are all genuine problems for Christians who may have had an inner change of life but now need to grow.

The prophet Isaiah (8:19) chides those who chirp and mutter. This may be meaningless talk. It may be talk just to talk. Whatever it might be called in its many variations, it is not fitting for the Christian.

In other words, it is not enough simply to avoid gross excesses of speech: lying, cursing, gossiping, and stirring up evil by excesses. All these are so very obvious.

Small decisions affect the whole of life. Stop chirping and muttering, just running at the mouth.

Roger Bannister, the famed miler, once said about sport and his running that it taught him the need to make decisions. No less is true for Christian living.

"Quick decisions are needed," he said. "Sport leads to self-discovery of limitations."

* * * * *

How would you at present evaluate the harmful effects of out-and-out lying and cheating?

Is it very much different from what may result from what is often called "a white lie?"

How much chirping and muttering do you do? How much do you hear from others? Decide how to stop.

5th Day — People With Discernment

I John 4:13-16

Kenneth Scott Latourette, the church historian, has pointed out two outstanding facts of the 20th century concerning Christianity. First, Christianity is today more widely distributed geographically and more deeply rooted among more people than it or any other faith has ever been.

By a strange and striking contrast, second, Christianity has never been as extensively challenged as in the twentieth century.

Latourette calls special attention to Communism as being one source of opposition.

Christians, it would seem, should be more alive, more aggressive and more forward-looking because of the opportunity given to them and because of the challenges of our day.

Yet, the reverse has happened. Perhaps the church has been spoiled by success. Nothing undermines like success.

Perhaps Christians have spent too much time trying to do as the world does - get people to like you and constantly conforming to things as they are instead of being transformed (Rom. 12:2).

To be transformed would be to have God live in us and have His love perfected in us (I Jn. 4:12).

In this way we might then become people with discernment and able to tell the differences between the holy and the profane and the clean and the unclean (Ezek. 44:23).

The challenge for Christians in our day has largely gone unheeded. Many have commented on it. Henry Sloan Coffin, Sr., pointed out many years ago that Americans have always been falsely self-reliant and too cocky.

Only penitent, pardoned, and truly humble Americans would do any good in the world. "We have not realized," wrote Coffin, "that in three-score years and ten, man does not pass much beyond this kindergarten stage."

Let God in. Let Him give you discernment.

* * * * *

Consider how you would describe your own discernment. Write it down. How can you improve?
How have you been self-defiant?
How does loving someone else tell you anything about the love of God?
How are wisdom and knowledge different?

6th Day — Hope for the Future

I John 4:17-21

"The only guide to a man for right and wrong is his conscience," is a statement with which many would agree. Yet when attempts are made to describe "conscience" there are sharp differences of opinion.

To most people conscience is a feeling of obligation to do right or be good, coupled with the uncomfortable feeling which follows if the evil is thought of or chosen instead of the good.

Conscience may be described as a power to decide as to the moral quality of one's own thoughts or acts. To many *conscience* is the *only guide* they have. *That is unfortunate.*

Christians need to recognize it as unfortunate because a conscience may be good for nothing if it is not an educated conscience.

We know and believe that God has sent Jesus into the world. God is love (I John 4:16) and whoever lives in love, God lives in him.

The only way a conscience can be educated is to have it possessed by the love of God, not fear. Perfect love casts out fear (IJohn 4:18).

The only hope for our future is to be possessed by and to be overcome by God's love and show it by not hating those we can see. How is it possible to hate him who can be seen and love God who cannot be seen (I John 4:19-20)?

There is nothing in man good of itself that does not need God to make it good. That is true of the fruits of the mind and the promptings of the conscience. Our only hope for the future is to awaken to this fact of life.

The conscience is a weak stick to lean on for our guidance. If the feelings of a man need to be turned in the right direction, so does the conscience. Yet many Christians still go on leaning for advice on their uneducated conscience.

Educate your conscience in the ways of the Word of God. Then you will be able to trust in it.

* * * * *

What is your definition of "conscience?" What is a "good conscience?" Do you disagree with the views of the meditation about conscience? How is "love" the answer to the future?

7th Day — Consider Well the Highway

Romans 7:4-12

Knowledge of a law is not enough to be able to follow it. It may be even the cause of breaking it. This kind of reasoning may be confusing at first, but follow Paul's argument in the 7th chapter of Romans.

The key directional signs on the highway that is to be traveled by the Christian are as follows: law, faith, sin, rebellion, and grace. It does not matter in what order they are placed. Life is not orderly for any of us, so the signs need to be heeded at any moment.

We tend more to sin and rebellion than to obedience. Law is easier to follow than to live by faith, for we deceive ourselves in thinking that our works save us. Grace is a love gift of God offered to all men whether they believe or not.

However, grace is not infused or engrafted (James 1:21) to one's soul's salvation until the heart is turned toward God.

God even helps us in the turning. He gives us power to handle our own rebellion and sin, our passions and conflict situations. Consider well the highway we must travel. Obey the signs.

Zeno, the Stoic philosopher, first brought out the notion of "human nature" in the 4th century B.C. He believed that the human soul is a detached piece of the divine nature, a piece that is imprisoned in a particular body.

If this be true, then it would follow that this piece of divine nature, since it shares that which is divine, would have certain innate ideas and qualities to it that would be helpful for man's guidance.

The reasoning would go like this: we are a piece of God, there is goodness in us, we can know goodness innately, and we need only bring it out in us.

In your growth toward Christian maturity be advised well that this thinking is a detour of heartaches. Follow God's highway spelled out in Scripture.

* * * * *

How much goodness is in our natures?

Is there a capacity in us to distinguish between good and evil ?

Does the educated or the uneducated person sin more? What have you observed?

When you consider the hate and violence which exist in the world and which are so much pictured and described for us constantly, it would be wise to be reconciled to two facts.

The first fact is that what is heard or seen about all of this is quite true. The second fact, which might be more difficult to accept, is that the fruits of hate do exist in us. Our frozen words may well produce hot deeds of destruction.

However, this reconciliation to the facts about human nature is gloriously broken by God's grace.

Decide to submit your life to Him.

PSALM 3

5 I lie down and sleep;
    I wake again, for the Lord sustains
      me.
6 I am not afraid of ten thousands of peo-
      ple
    who have set themselves against me
      round about.

THE SIXTH WEEK
A CHRISTIAN STANCE

Introductory Bible reading for this week:
2 Peter 2:4-10

Hostility fills the pages of the Bible. Man is hostile to God. Cain kills his brother Abel. Joseph's brothers are jealous of him and sell him into slavery. Jezebel hates the prophet Elijah.

The hostility of the Pharisees and Sadducees against Jesus is one of the earmarks of the four Gospels. Paul met hostile crowds wherever he went.

The Holy Scriptures in this connection mirrors life in every age, including our own. Hostility is irrational. It leads to violence.

A force so powerful needs a counterforce. Love contends against hostility, the love of God through Christ Jesus.

Find the proper Christian stance in this world. See the rainbow through the rain. God sustains.

1st Day — Day of the Lord

Matthew 24:36-44

"The world is coming to an end!" is a warning cry heard in every generation. Christians have often lent their zeal to end-of-the-world jitters.

In 595 A.D., Gregory the Great cried out, "It is the last hour: Pestilence and sword are raging the whole world. Nation is rising against nation, the whole fabric of things is being shaken."

In the year 1,000 everybody was sure that that was the end. In the last century in the United States the Millerites were sure of the end of the world.

From these examples, some would ridicule a belief in Scriptural views about the end of time. The "Day of the Lord" just is not rational, they would argue.

A distinction must be made between predicting specifically when the world will end and holding the view that some day the world will end.

Many evangelists, past and present, have walked into the trap of predicting the hour, the day, the month and the year for the world's end. The Bible, from which they claim they have received this revelation, is a book they only partially read.

Jesus spoke of the end of the world. He likened it to the day of Noah, but Jesus' stress was on preparation for the end, not on the time of the end: "Watch therefore," Jesus said, "for you do not know on what day your Lord is coming (Mt. 24:42)."

Certainly the Bible contains the view that some day the world will end, and all men will be judged.

As you face hostility, as you hear about wars and rumors of wars (Mk. 13:7), do not be troubled.

There is a Christian posture and stance which must be taken. The great tragedy is that by dismissing specific predictions as absurd, we may also dismiss valid teachings.

We must understand the Day of the Lord in terms of the promise of God of eternal victory.

* * * * *

Why did Noah continue to build the ark in spite of the evidence against him?

What do you regard as the proper stance for the Christian to take about the end of the world?

What underlying error do you think people make who continue to predict the immediate end of the world?

2nd Day — Pass Through Waters

Matthew 24:45-51

None can conclude that love of the Lord will prevent their having to pass through difficult times. God does not promise us no problems, but he promises to be with us always.

This then is another aspect of the Christian stance, to face unafraid life's upsets. Consider the promise from the words of the prophet Isaiah (43:2): "When you pass through waters, I will be with you; and through the rivers, they shall not overflow you; when you walk through the fire, you shall not be burned, and the flame shall not consume you."

But faithfulness is required for the Christian stance. "Blessed is that servant," Jesus says, who is found doing good to his household (Mt. 24:45-46), when his Lord returns.

The fact that days are evil and it looks as though, as every generation has concluded, the days are prolonged and every vision fails (Ezek. 12:22) is no excuse for faithlessness.

Noah faced this problem but still did according to everything that the Lord commanded him to do (Gen. 7:5). It must have been a temptation for Noah, in the midst of his generation's preoccupation with evil, to question God's directions. However, it is not doubting and questioning which is sin. It is the lingering and turning over the tempting possibilities and dwelling on them to prepare to do them which is sinful.

The thoughts that pass through one's mind are not sinful in themselves. Many people worry needlessly over such things. You cannot be blamed, an old story goes, for the birds which might come and rest on your head. You can be blamed, however, if you let them build nests in your hair. So it is with fleeting thoughts. Do not let them stay.

God's promises are valid now as always.

* * * * *

Have you noted a pattern in your life of direction in spite of your failures? Describe it.

Turn to Hebrews 11:1, read it, and relate it to this day's meditation in terms of another aspect of a Christian stance.

Are you living practically by faith daily?

3rd Day — Fluttering Birds

Matthew 25:1-13

Everybody wants to be improved but no one wants to change. All of us want to have sweeter dispositions, controlled tempers, better manners, and a greater capacity to master various skills.

Such people are like fluttering birds - lots of agitation going nowhere.

Now when there are clear reasons for changing in order to improve and a person keeps on doing only what he has done in the past, would you not call such a person a foolish person?

The parable of the ten virgins is like that. Five of them prepared. Five did not prepare. Of course the five who did not prepare had to be called foolish. They were not ready when the bridegroom, Christ, returned. Jesus gives direct, brief, but profound advice: "Watch (Mt. 25:13)."

Churches would like to improve but no one wants to change. There are only two ways that the church could change for the better. One way would be some new terrifying persecution of the church which would rid it of the status-seekers, the deadwood who enjoy the club atmosphere, and are comfort-seekers.

Somehow, though the warnings are constant, no will listen, prepare, and be ready. The Lord said to the people of Israel through Amos: "Woe to those who are at ease in Zion (6:1)." "Zion", a hill in Jerusalem, was a name used to indicate "the church of God," "the people of Israel," and sometimes "heaven."

The second way the church could change would be through the actions of one person, one who would be willing to carve through the murky varnish of apathy which overlays so many churches. Yes, one could do it. You could be that one where you live, in your place. The church needs you where you are!

However, we should not lose sight of the fact that God has anticipated reformations. There is One, Christ, who once-for-all, did what needed to be done for mankind and for the church.

So Christ leads. You and I follow, one added to one person, to one person. Ready and willing!

* * * * *

What place does the Church have in God's plan for the future?
What is the place of the individual Christian in the Church?
Why must we say that the two are needed and complement each other, the individual and the group?

4th Day — Noisy One

Luke 19:12-27

Giving may be done without faith. Faith or trust may have nothing to do with giving. One may give to self. One may have faith only in self.

When Abraham was willing to sacrifice, as he would a lamb, his son Isaac (Gen. 22:1-18), it was Abraham's giving-faith that God rewarded. Jesus spoke of faith in God the Father. Out of that faith he gave to many who were ill the gift of healing and of faith.

Faith is a conviction of belief - belief that something must be done with what one is given. The wicked servant in the parable did a lot of talking but showed no faith and did not trust in giving so he would receive.

Egypt was once called a "noise" by Jeremiah (46:17). The term would seem to be very applicable to the servant who kept the pound given to him laid in a napkin and who hurried to explain his inactivity (Lk. 19:20-21). The "noisy one" with lots of words but no actions - no faith in the future and no willingness to give.

That servant no doubt would have liked to have been among those rewarded for increasing their Lord's wealth. He probably wanted to improve his lot in life, but he was not willing to take the proper Christian stance. That stance, in this instance, was proper stewardship of what was given to him.

Just as with every disciple, change has to begin with proper evaluation and then a decision to trust in God.

A proper evaluation concludes that, through God's help, we must fight and struggle to change. It comes no other way. We must pray to God to aid us to move when we would rather stay put.   It was Martin Luther, the German reformer, who described the Christian as one who "does not stand still." The life in faith implies, in Luther's words, "progress, a walk or journey toward heaven into another life." No retracing steps or standing still.

When Ezekiel wrote about the ordinances of the temple, he gave good advice for us all about life too: go out a different gate from the one you came in (Ezek. 46:9). Do not go over the same ground constantly. Break new ground.

* * * * *

What implications do you find for your own faith in the view that if you live to yourself you will die to yourself?

What talents do you have which have actually been lost through misuse?

5th Day — Not Returned Empty

Matthew 25:31-40

Asking to be excused is common to life. In good faith we accept a dinner invitation or say we are willing to plan a program for a Sunday church school class, and promise to meet a friend under the old clock at the railroad station.

Unexpected or forgotten responsibilities arise, we may get sick, or we change our minds completely about wanting to fulfill our obligation.

We ask to be excused. An excuse may be valid or it may be simply a flimsy excuse or subterfuge. The real reason may not be given either from embarrassment or from unwillingness to hurt the feelings of others.

Life is filled with reasons for making excuses. One of them relates to serving others. If a man says he loves God and hates his brother, he is a liar (I John 4:20). The two go hand in hand.

If one loves God, he will love others - if his love for God is genuine.

God extends the invitation to engage in the work of the Kingdom. There are two common deterrents to accepting the invitation. First, it is possible to confuse the acceptance of God's invitation with the words, "Come, follow me, and join my church."

The invitation is not to join a church but to commit oneself to God and His cause. There has been far too much emphasis on joining, having one's name on the church rolls.

However, the common sharing is necessary. The strong-minded individual is needed everywhere, especially in the church. When a ship is close enough to the pier for docking, a hawser is thrown. The hawser is made up of single ropes and each is made up of many single strands. The creaking of the hawser shows the great weight put on it, but it holds. So do Christians banded together when one might be weak. Each serves the other, or should.

Each is rewarded or punished according to service.

* * * * *

If we are justified by faith not works, then how does it follow that service to others seems to be counted by Jesus as very important?

What excuses do you give for putting off service to others?

Is society too large to serve the individual?

6th Day - Double Destruction

Matthew 25:41-46

The second deterrent to accepting the invitation to engage in the work of God's Kingdom is to look at things too personally.

Our own problems may create weariness, despondency, uncertainty, frustration, and confusion. We do not want to be disturbed. We do not want to be involved. We wish other people would leave us alone.

A certain amount of this is natural. However, when it becomes excessive, when a person reacts to all of life in this manner, one should pause. There may well be good cause for a person to pull himself up short and ask some serious questions.

Why do I react this way to everything?

Have I been carrying a great health problem without being aware of it? Many people fear finding out if they are ill, when by their delay in finding out they may be getting worse.

No one wants to be a hypochondriac - rushing to the doctor at any abnormal or unusual symptom. But many people are prevented from enjoying the thrills of normal life by carelessness regarding their own health.

One might add, sometimes a problem which may appear to be a faith-problem is really a health problem.

When there are no problems of this type, then there are very serious consequences for the disciple who neglects his responsibilities.

It still happens in mission lands that confession of belief in Christ means for the convert to be cast out by his family. Gainful employment may be difficult if not impossible. Fortunately, in Christian lands this rarely happens.

The punishment of which Christ speaks, everlasting punishment (Mt. 25:46), may strike the modern believer as exaggeration. Who can *prove* there is a hell? Or a heaven? Take no one's word for punishment. But do believe in the Word.

* * * * *

Is illness a form of punishment by God? Do not answer either yes or no without going deeper.

What is meant by having life and having it abundantly?

Do you believe there is a hell?

7th Day — Day of Evil

Romans 14:10-19

There will be a day of reckoning for us all. God gives good gifts, but each must face also His judgment.

Many centuries ago a Biblical writer observed, "Where there is no vision, the people perish (Prov. 29:18)." This is the King James' version.

Would it seem that the vision is the key, not the works, that determines the judgement of God? Perhaps so. Where does one get a vision best? On the housetop? On top of the mountain?

One might think vision comes best with a mountain top experience, high and lifted up, close to the heavens, away from all the clamor of daily life.

No, not so. When one is most down, when discouragement seems most to take over to smother all creative hope - when one is in the valley of prejudice, or anger, or captivity, then the vision is most likely to come.

The Prodigal was at his lowest point when he came to himself (Luke 15:17). Saul found God on the way to Damascus where he went breathing threats and murder against the disciples of the Lord (Acts 9:1).

There was a modern woman once who failed in everything she tried to do. She even failed to commit suicide. She said, "It is a shameful realization to discover that you cannot even do a good job in taking your own life."

She was her own worst enemy. In the valley of her life a vision overcame her - no, God came over her and converted her. Her heart was remade.

You may be saying, "I have never been that down and out." Has it ever occurred to you that you may be among the thousands who are *up* and *out*. All of us are sometimes.

We are *up* on normal living, but very much *out* of God's way. Now maybe it is good to be *out* of other people's way - but not God's.

* * * * *

At this moment where do you stand so far as God is concerned? Are you out of it?

Does God really need to punish us directly?

What is your present stance as a Christian?

There are many wonderful places on the face of the earth. There are fertile valleys and high-reaching mountains. There are fine people everywhere.

Still, where we are is where we must grow and change. There is need in our land to create a people who have a chance to look at the mistakes made in the past and build to avoid making them again. We must help in God's new creation.

We must be a light for others, to guide them. Yet, are we good enough? Has our unbridled freedom destroyed us? God says, if my people will humble themselves, I will forgive and heal (II Chron. 7:14).

PROVERBS 28

26 He who trusts in his own mind is a fool.

THE SEVENTH WEEK
A WAY AND A WILL

Introductory Bible reading for this week:
Isaiah 14:3-15

"Where there's a will, there's a way."

This common expression suggests a determined person, one who sets his mind on a seemingly impossible goal and by grit, ingenuity, and determination conquers all obstacles and reaches his goal.

There is a school of thought which states that nothing is impossible, and I do not refer to the Scriptural advice (Lk. 17:20) of Jesus. There God is the prime mover.

There are some things one cannot do. Years ago a thinker characterized Americans as people who mount horses and try to go off in all directions at the same time. You cannot bring back a loved one who has died.

To say that man has inexhaustible will power often simply shows pride and arrogance. There is another way.

1st Day — The Stagnant Waters

Luke 12:13-21

At one point in his narrative Sholem Asch has Paul say in *The Apostle:* "From this day forward my life shall be as the assaulting ocean."

This was after Paul had been found of God; there is pictured here the restless sea always in motion. Such a life is striving and active. It is one which is humble before God.

Stagnant waters, on the other hand, are the breeding place of disease because there is no flow or movement out of or away from self. Pride rules and foolishness results.

Jesus does not teach his disciples that it is wrong either to want or to have material possessions. He does teach, however, that no man can serve two masters (Mt. 6:24). Possessions are not the issue. The issue is where one's heart is, what is most important.

A rich man in the parable told by Luke (12:13-21) was guilty of placing his trust in his possessions. He was guilty of pride and therefore piling up treasure for himself and was not rich before God.

The wrong use of the will is destructive. We work harder and press toward destructive paths. It is not the goals which are wrong but the pathways we travel to accomplish them. We deepen selfishness, or we may get bitter toward life. Or, we submit to the natural man, saying, "After all, I am only human."

In other words this is an excuse to do anything we wish by any means just so long as we get where we want to go.

A British monk by the name of Pelagius went to the city of Rome in the year 400 A.D. He was distressed at the low state of conduct he saw there. He believed there was need for more energy and greater moral effort on the part of Christians especially.

Pelagius certainly believed, "Where there's a will, there's a way." Was Pelagius right or wrong? Augustine reacted against what he considered Pelagius' false theology. The issue is still before us today.

* * * * *

What are some ways that your will appears to have power to act?
What is the source of this power you believe you have to do as you wish?
What are the things you cannot in any way possibly change, though you may will them very much?

2nd Day — The Tossing Sea

Amos 6:8-14

The threatening of Amos against the people of Israel is neither idle nor vindictive. He states the truth not just as he sees it but as it had been revealed to him and then confirmed by his knowledge, observations, and experiences.

Faith is not going it blind, as many critics say. Faith, when acted upon, presents its overwhelming proofs as the days and years go by. This is really what Augustine and Pelagius argued about many centuries ago. Some of the issues are just as valid today as they were then.

For example, Pelagius was shocked by the prayer of Augustine in his *Confessions:* "Give what Thou commandest, and command what Thou wilt."

To Pelagius, Augustine's submission to the will of God seemed to deny to human beings the responsibility of their actions.

Pelagius denied that man had an inherited disposition to sin or that mankind was actually sinful, while Augustine on the basis of Scriptural evidence and his own and others' experiences confirmed both.

"Spineless foolishness," would have been the words Pelagius might have used about confession of sins. Pelagius stressed human responsibility for what happens. God has given man the capacity to solve his own problems by cooperating with the grace of God. There is something appealing and very modern about Pelagius' theology. Man is like a tossing sea and restless.

After all, man is not a puppet on a string. Surely, he has power to act and react. In practical affairs, you cannot expect God to answer and solve that which is properly in man's own hands.

Sometimes all of us tend to dismiss in history these past discussions and arguments of Christians. We say, "I do not have an academic background. Theology is out of my line."

It is foolish not to pay attention to these arguments from the past. They present to us matters which can save us personal grief. We can learn from them.

*   *   *   *   *

Why should we not read about past controversies in the church?
Did they not argue about Scripture and is not Scripture a concern of ours?
Assuming the correctness of the views of Pelagius so far, how would you support him further?

3rd Day - Worms Are Your Covering

Isaiah 14:3-15

Certainly the prophets cannot be said to fail to speak quite plainly. Isaiah says in effect to his people in countless ways, "You had it coming to you because you failed to continue your love to God. He delivered us from Egypt. Now he uses other nations as the hand of his wrath. Will we never learn?" Isaiah says, "Maggots and worms cover you (14:11)." No question about his meaning, is there?

Apparently every generation must be taught the facts about the moral life. Nothing can be taken for granted. The lessons go back to the beginning.

Man's aspirations often are practised in defiance of God foolishly, as in the efforts to build the tower of Babel (Gen. 11:1-9). So progressively men keep making the same mistakes, especially presuming that they can stand in the place of God.

Augustine, in the prayer which had so offended Pelagius, had also prayed, "I have no hope at all but in thy great mercy."

It was at the point of man's free will that the issue was joined between Pelagius and Augustine.

Augustine believed that grace is a free gift, given by God without which none can be saved. We receive love from God without willing it ourselves. Grace cannot be earned. Who earns a gift? Grace, Augustine said, is a "secret, wonderful and ineffable power operating within," through which God works in men's hearts not only revelations of truth and wisdom but also the moulding and turning of the will.

We must give up our wills to God's will. What follows is the spirit of grace which causes us to have faith in order that through faith we may, on praying for an increase of it, obtain the ability to do what God commands.

On the other side, Pelagius would have said in effect: "Of course there's a will, yours. Use it. Hammer away at it.Use it to determine what you want."

Submit to God's will. There is no other way.

* * * * *

Is there truth on both sides of the controversy known as the Pelagian controversy?
How would Paul's views in Romans 7:19 side with Augustine?
How can you make your will really free?

4th Day — The Issues of Life

Mark 7:14-23

In this Markan passage Jesus spells out the source of evil and his view of "human nature." He agreed fully with the writer of Proverbs, "Keep your heart with all vigilance; for from it flow the springs of life (4:23)."

Jesus' position here runs counter to all modern dominant views of our day. Jesus says that there is *nothing outside* which can defile a man (Mk. 7:5). Many thinkers today would place blame on forces *outside* of man for man's predicaments, saying man *inside* is good.

When Jesus says that from within, out of the heart of men, come all evil things (Mk. 7:21-23), he would also face the contradiction of many modern thinkers. They would say, "Nonsense. Man basically is very good. He needs simply love, kindness, and direction for that goodness to come out."

There is great persuasiveness in such arguments. They are very congenial to what we want to believe about ourselves. What is persuasive, or held by the majority, however, is not necessarily the truth. Sin, in ideas and in form, is not the ugly distortion we often imagine. It is mostly appealing and beautiful. If this were not so, what would be the power of any temptation?

At the commencement exercises of a large Southern university, the poem *Invictus*, by William E. Henley was sung. It followed the invocation and was meant no doubt to provide a religious tone to the gathering.

Instead, it revealed a proud man shaking a clenched fist at God. One may properly regard the poem as representative of much modern thinking and a reaction to Jesus' thought just described. Henley wrote:

> Out of the night which covers me,
> Black as the Pit from pole to pole,
> I thank whatever gods may be
> For my unconquerable soul.

The familiar lines in a later stanza are: "I am the master of my fate: I am the captain of my soul."

The contrast here is very obvious. Choose.

* * * * *

The lines are drawn sharply between Jesus' views and modern views. Are they exaggerated?

Do evil things come out of a baby's heart?

Reflect on your life. Do you find that what Jesus says is true in your experience?

How do ideas affect actions practically?

5th Day — He Rules By Love

Matthew 5:1-10

The idea of the evil inclination of the heart is not only meaningful and true but empirically verifiable. "Confession is good for the soul," is a profound truism.

It is a relief to step down from the pedestal of thinking of ourselves as gods. Confessional prayer cauterizes and thereby heals the wounds that our self-will has inflicted.

God rules us by love, but we must understand the reality of sin and evil. More than that, it must be taught to the young so they understand fully what it is that life holds. It is only when one realizes how prevalent evil is that one understands the true power of genuine goodness. "Evil cannot exist without good," writes St. Augustine in *The City of God.*

The beginning of pride is when we turn from God. Pride is the beginning of sin.

It is impudent to proclaim the goodness of human nature so long as children are hungry in the world, prejudice rules men's hearts, and there are evil impulses in the minds of men.

"Rend your hearts, and not your garments. Return to the Lord, your God," the prophet Joel writes, "for he is gracious and merciful, slow to anger, and abounding in steadfast love, and repents of evil (2:13)."

"Blessed," Jesus says of those who are of this frame of mind - "happy" is another translation of the Greek. The frame of mind is that of the repentent, the humble of heart, the meek, the merciful, and the peacemakers.

The appeal of a poem like *Invictus,* though contrary to Jesus' teachings, is understandable. Man is exalted. Powers would crush him. He rebels and fights back, as though saying, "Will me the will to keep me unconquered even when my head is bloody."

It takes a great deal of faith to hold such a view as this. It takes faith also to be a man or woman of non-Christian faith.

But there is a better way. A better way by far!

* * * * *

How might you justify the "chip on the shoulder" attitude toward life?
What are the ways to deal with human needs which people feel cannot be met by turning to God?
Are such people correct in their assumptions?
Are any areas beyond God's capacity to enter?

6th Day — Builders Outstrip Destroyers

Matthew 5:21-26

One church leader has characterized Americans as having articles of faith in science (in its engineering applications), common sense (his own ideas), the Golden Rule (in its negative form), sportsmanship, and individual independence.

This faith he further characterizes as follows: "He believes in God but his god is not to be confused with a transcendent being to whom he owes duty and life itself, but rather his god is a combination of whipping boy, servant and even a useful ally in dealing with religious people, who otherwise might get in his way."

There is a man! There is a will and a way!

How can such a person ever admit that he has sinned against his brother, as Jesus suggests (Mt. 5:23)?

How could he ever admit he needed reconciliation? Perhaps more important, what do we do with such persons when we honestly try to be reconciled with them and they refuse in cases of disagreements?

Jesus tells us to forgive seven times seventy (Mt. 18:22). He also tells us to go to our brother, then take two witnesses along if he refuses to listen. Then tell it to the church, then reject him if he will not listen to the church (Mt. 18:15-17.).

Then what? There is still a proper way under the guidance of God's will. It is based upon the assumption that builders of the Kingdom will outlast those who destroy the Kingdom.

Sentimentality alone is folly when conflict and hostility exist. First, a builder believes that reconciliation is desirable and necessary. Second, he believes there should be an open heart *and* mind, to hear, to feel, to reason, to talk, and to share.

"Oh, forget the issues involved and make up," is the common approach of sentimentality.

The resistant mind must first be heart-directed before it can become reason-directed. You cannot stop loving and forgiving, but it takes time to convert others. Some never are.

* * * * *

How is this meditation related to one of Jesus' teachings about not casting your pearls before swine (Mt. 7:6)?

Does this require more knowledge than we are capable of achieving?

7th Day — Too Weary To Repent

Matthew 5:38-48

In Jesus' teaching in this portion of the Sermon on the Mount, one finds the utmost kindness and thoughtfulness ever suggested by Jesus. We are to love our enemies, bless those who curse us, do good to those who hate us, and pray for those who despitefully use us (Mt. 5:44).

This is another example of Jesus fulfilling the law by going one step beyond it. This is really acting against pride.

Paul in writing to the Ephesians underscores all these admonitions, saying in part, "Be kind to one another, tenderhearted, forgiving one another. (Eph. 4:31-32)."

In the face of practical circumstances which face us and in terms of genuine hostilities in which we may be fully involved, these teachings may be very abrasive and appear impossible.

We may wish to resist, saying, "Impractical, irrelevant, and unrealistic." Or, we may be worn out from the conflict. We may be too worn out to repent. But, if we are too worn out to repent, so may be our opponent too.

Only the converted Christian could possibly stand on such teachings and genuinely try to follow them. One might just as well talk to the statue in the park or the toaster on the table as to talk to the unconverted man or woman about hostilities and the way out.

At least the toaster is connected to some live current. The unconverted (therefore, the uncommitted to God and the Kingdom) are connected to nothing but self and closed up by self.

The converted must love, forgive, do good as he is able, and put aside all bitterness, wrath, and clamor - *so far as it depends on him*. He must always have the door open to reconciliation. Jesus means what He says. This is His will and His way.

Neglect not, however, the whole armor of God for we fight in a hostile and perverse world (Eph. 6:10-17).

* * * * *

Does Scripture teach us to desire and strive for peace at any price?
What are some of the issues worth continuing to fight for?
How do you keep alive your capacity to forgive?

If men would realize the power of faith, then the whole world would change. The world will not change with the ideas we have - our wills and our ways.

When change takes place, in ourselves and in others, it is caused by the common denominator men find when they deal in the higher circles of God's work and life within them.

Consider, however, the course of life of Jesus and men like Paul and Augustine, two of his prominent disciples, and relate their controversies to your own. Make sure that you retain the capacity to be humble, while holding your opinions.

PSALM 18

16 He reached from on high, he took
    me,
  he drew me out of many waters.

THE EIGHTH WEEK
THE BRIDGE TO COURAGE

Introductory Bible reading for this week:
Romans 4:13-25

In its practice of religion and the picture of religion presented to its members and the world, the organized church has often failed to meet the practical needs of men and women.

Authority has often been substituted for religious experience. Emotionalism has often been confused with faith.

Christianity is or should be a reforming and upsetting force in the world. But this is only characteristic of thoroughgoing Christians. What about the rest of us? Halford E. Luccock observes about Christians, "Why, we wouldn't upset a teacup!"

The world cries for moral leadership. The church gives platitudes. The world cries for bread. The church gives a stone. Needed is the bridge to courage.

1st Day — A Promise Believed

Hebrews 11:8-12

Courage is needed in our land.

"There is fear in the land," says one observer. "Men and women are worried sick about their skins and their earthly goods."

"I'm confused and afraid," says a parent, "not so much for myself as for my children."

The above comments are no doubt true for many people. But we seem actually to be worried more about lack of leadership and aimlessness in community and world affairs. Out of these fears, or lacks, come the frightening and discouraging feeling of uselessness.

For more than half a century we have been living in a barren no-man's land of confusion of past values compared with present realities that are disruptive, chaotic, and apparently irrational.

To turn to lessons about a man like Abraham may seem a far cry from our need for courage. What can a man thousands of years dead tell us about our complex modern world, a far cry from his nomadic world?

He can tell us at least one thing - believe in the promises of God. He did. So have thousands since his day up to the present time. There is proof piled upon proof.

It is difficult, especially when faced with aimlessness, to believe in the future. There is no chart to follow for the immediate steps of faith of moving from the known to the unknown will of God.

However, it is the only way. Obviously we need a new faith, a faith which gives us real courage. Talking about a surface faith is worse than no answer. Tell that to the parents who have just lost a lovely curly-headed youngster. Slap the father on the back and say the magic formula, "Have faith."

The Christian church has itself to blame for much of the loss of faith in our day. The Biblical message has not properly been geared to adults.

*   *   *   *   *

What are some of the criticisms you can level at the organized church today?
How do you think we should go about finding the courage needed today?
How would you respond to the criticism that the past is the past and has no relevance now?

2nd Day — Sweet As Honey

Hebrews 11:17-19

Abraham was willing to go all the way with faith. There was nothing halfhearted. He was willing to sacrifice his son, Isaac, when he believed God wanted him to do so.

Apart now from the issues of whether God really wanted Isaac's death or that Abraham may simply have *thought* he was doing God's will, what could have happened to Abraham to be willing to go as far as that?

First, something big. There are two kinds of faith. One is assenting to something that it is or probably is so. The second is staking one's life on the fact that what is believed to be true is *actually* true. So Abraham had the second kind of faith and it was something big in his life.

We do not know exactly how to describe his experience of God but we do know the results of it. It could have been something similar to that described by Ezekiel when he was instructed by the Lord to eat the words of a holy book, a roll: "Then I ate it; and it was in my mouth as sweet as honey (3:1-3)."

For Abraham, second, what happened to him was all-pervasive. He did not regard what had happened to him as a once-a-week concern.

Third, Abraham regarded the source of what had happened to him as being God, and for God he would hold nothing back.

Our world has for a long time been counting on faith in science to answer our problems for us and to give us a bridge to courage. There has been an uneasiness about this as an answer since World War II when science did not produce the atmosphere required.

The spell has been broken. The way is now prepared for the setting up of questions without answers.

At least the answers are known not to be known. This opens the way for honest searching for new ways to deal with the common problems of mankind.

* * * * *

What defense would you present that Christian faith is not blind groping?
How is the past a guide to the future, if you think it is? If not, where would you look for guides to present and future answers?

3rd Day — Love Never Ceases

Romans 4:1-8

When Paul writes in Romans that Abraham believed God, and it was counted to him for righteousness (4:3) what actually is Paul saying to us?

Let us begin by suggesting what Paul does *not* mean. Paul does not mean faith gave Abraham anything. Faith could be faith in self or faith in faith. A popular song some years ago seemed to many to be a religious song because the lyrics had the words, "I believe." The lyrics never did state in what the singer believed. He just believed!

What Paul tells us about Abraham can perhaps best be described by saying that Abraham *believed in the love of God.* It is not faith. It is not hope. It is love. Paul writes, "So faith, hope, love abide, these three; but the greatest of these is love (I Cor. 13:13)."

About this love Paul also writes that it never ceases (I Cor. 13:8).

If this is related to the need for a bridge to courage, that bridge can only be the love of God.

Some churches fail miserably to teach religion because they try entertainment to entice people into the fellowship of Christ's followers. The stress there is *only believe,* a stress no better than the one-time modern song.

Other churches present flavorless diets of timeworn cliches with the hope that through much repetition of Biblical phrases the listener will eventually succumb. He perhaps does succumb. He dies a spiritual death, if he has the lack of character to stick it out week after week.

Some leave the church entirely, perhaps out of honest integrity to their own standards of rational thought. They may even accept this experience as normal.

Every church, no matter what the style or content, today has to be challenged to its best. The end result may be, unless the churches awaken, the loss of souls who have faith, no love, no courage — and, eventually, no church.

* * * * *

How would you go about implementing the understanding of the kind of faith stressed here?

What is the responsibility of the lay people to encourage their clergy toward more courage?

What is the responsibility of the clergy toward the laity to speak to the needs of the times?

4th Day — The Christian Never Arrives

Romans 4:9-12

Paul stresses an important but simple fact: Abraham's faith in the love of God is valid for Jew and Gentile alike. He is the father of all them that believe (Rom. 4:11), but it is very apparent that Abraham grows from faith to faith.

There is progress in Abraham's faith, though once-for-all in the beginning he was justified, as Hebrews 11 makes quite clear.

"He who through faith is righteous shall live (Rom. 1:17) is true doctrine, justification by faith. Some Christians add the word "alone." However, this is unbiblical and theologically inadequate for our day.

"Faith alone" meant in the past to exclude works as being sufficient for justification and also to exclude any combination of faith *and* works.

Today, the idea of faith alone leads to overconfidence. The Christian never arrives.

In this world a goal is set and achieved. To believe something is final, at an end, is to live as the world lives. It is not the way a Christian lives.

So long as there is a prayer which has not been prayed, so long as there is a passage of Scripture which has not been long pondered over, the Christian goes on learning and growing and maturing in faith.

It is obvious then that the work is never done. A Christian never really ever arrives. He might arrive so far as accomplishments of points along the line is concerned, and it is good to have them. But he never arrives to stay.

He thinks immediately of another trip. He pauses only to start out afresh. His faith expands.

It is no wonder that Moses had the people of Israel in the wilderness for forty years for growth and preparation. They needed it.

Today we need a revival of the concept of never-ending goals. For too many years Christians have rested on laurels won. The reckoning is upon us.

*   *   *   *   *

What daring is required not to settle down into established routine?
What are some of the ramifications of never arriving for day to day work for the Christian?
How can you help others to understand this?

5th Day — A Harvest in the Land

Romans 4:13-15

Analyzing the American scene many years ago, one thinker wrote: "The present state of America is truly alarming to every man who is capable of reflection . . . the mind of the multitude is left at random, and seeing fixed objects before them, they pursue such as fancy and opinion starts . . . wherefore, everyone thinks himself to act as he pleases."

These words were written by an American patriot, published in the year 1776, and titled, "A Call for Independence."

They show how problems remain from age to age, for they certainly reflect our age.

There is in our land a people ripe for harvesting to an understanding of righteousness through faith (Rom. 4:13). For most of these people their view of religion is the law of "don'ts". Do not do this or that. That is their association with religion.

To establish the bridge of courage for them means the renewal of Christians to understand their own faith. Certainly the law is our heritage. Certainly we stand where the people of Israel stood on the values of the Ten Commandments. But we are able ministers of the new testament, "Not in a written code, but in the Spirit; for the written code kills, but the Spirit gives life (II Cor. 3:6)."

If we make legalistic demands on new converts, then how are we different from those who, in the early church, made similar demands upon Gentiles that they follow every letter of the Jewish law before they could become Christian?

Not different at all.

Someone has written, "Faith and freedom are the two most important aspects of man's fundamental need: Love. Where love reigns, faith and freedom follow. When love dies, faith and freedom die also."

It is our love of God people need, not our laws.

* * * * *

What distinction should exist between the Christian and the non-Christian?
What is the best approach to introduce Christ to someone who has little knowledge of Him?
Why would you say love is, in the long run, a harder taskmaster than the law?

6th Day — Enlarge Your Tent

Romans 4:16-25

A prominent Jewish rabbi once indicated that if he were a Christian as he was a Jew, he would think more highly of the people from whom Jesus came than Christians normally do.

How true an observation is this? We are the inheritors of the tradition of Abraham, Isaac, and Jacob.

We are because of Abraham the children of promise. He is our spiritual father.

For too many years Christians have lived in a narrow house of thought and life. To use a biblical term, it is time for Christians to enlarge their tents (Is. 54:2). While we are people of the New Covenant, we rest on the old. If the Scriptures of the New Testament quite properly could be called the head, then the Old Testament is the body. One is not complete without the other.

If, then, we can include the people of Abraham, how much more should we not include those who call on the name of Christ? Our tent should be larger still.

After the colonists had gained their independence from England through the Revolutionary War, the Virginia legislature in 1785 passed an "Act for Establishing Religious Freedom."

All religious groups were made equal before the law. Other states followed Virginia's example, and the same principle was expressed in the first amendment to the United States Constitution.

This principle does not separate the State from God, from ethical and moral principles, or the exercise of the influence of religion on the state, the officials of government, and the people of this country.

No freedom for self is worth much unless it is coupled with freedom for others. This is another plank in the bridge to courage.

*   *   *   *   *

In what way could we call Abraham the spiritual father of the believing Christian?

Why would you say Christians are committed to defend the right of others to worship according to the dictates of their consciences?

7th Day — A New Heart

Romans 5:1-5

The love of God through Jesus Christ gives us a new heart. There is no courage without heart. The Holy Spirit gives us enlightenment, and our hope is made full (Rom. 5:4-5).

Christians ought to lead others to new hearts, for all our countrymen.

Thomas Jefferson once declared, "I have sworn upon the altar of God eternal hostility against every form of tyranny over the mind of men."

The reason for concern in our day for our nation's welfare is that every condition which hinders the common good today hinders the good of the Christian Church.

Besides, Christians are needed in a special way in today's society to be what Jesus called the leaven of his kingdom (Mt. 13;13).

The first special need is the guarantee of the right of difference of opinion in the sphere of religion.

The second special need is right of freedom to win believers for all religious groups, limited only by the protection that force may not be used and unlawful influences may not be practised.

The third special need is to continue to keep any one church from dominating our government in any official or diplomatic capacity. Democracy best combats any force of moral totalitarianism by insisting itself on the continued separation of church and state.

The fourth special need is to encourage influences between church and state as desirable and necessary. There is, moreover, a duty and responsibility of citizens to call government to task for violations of moral principles in official acts or by elected servants of the people.

Finally, there is a special need for freedom in our land: "For freedom Christ has set us free; stand fast therefore, and do not submit again to a yoke of slavery (Gal. 5:1)."

* * * * *

Should churches in official capacities attempt to influence legislation in the state or national level? Should the church ever espouse one candidate over another?

What duties are required of Christians to exercise toward the state?

Courage is an intangible quality. Yet it is a quality all Christians ought to possess and also ought help others to know.

Jesus Christ moved daily over the bridge of courage from faith to faith. He was not hurried. He was quite deliberate, even though he walked toward His own end. He chose to go to Jerusalem and was willing to die on a hill called Golgatha.

"This is His last journey. His life is now at an end," his enemies must have reasoned.

The Cross was not the end of life, Jesus' or ours. For Him and for us it meant only a new beginning.

PSALM 69

Save me, O God!
For the waters have come up to
my neck.

THE NINTH WEEK
THE MIDDLE OF THE ROAD

Introductory Bible reading for this week:
I Corinthians 10:6-13

Christianity is no middle of the road way of life, a fact easier to say than to practice day after day in the world where everything pleads for compromise.

Elijah challenged the people of Israel in a time of crisis, as this day is for us, "How long will you go limping with different two opinions? If the Lord is God, follow him; but if Baal, then follow him (I Kings 18:21)."

The difficulty of the decision, since it is not always clearcut exactly what to do, is revealed by the closing sentence of that same verse: "And the people did not answer him a word."

Jesus put it squarely: "He who is not with me is against me (Mt. 12:30)."

1st Day — No Extremism

I Corinthians 10:1-5

Experience *seems* to teach us that the middle of the road is not only valid but actually necessary in some circumstances. So Abram and Lot separated because Abram gave Lot the choice of the land for himself to settle a dispute (Gen. 13:8-13).

Lot's choice included the cities of Sodom and Gemorrah, which were destroyed, and Lot's wife was turned into a pillar of salt (Gen. 19:24-26).

The Genesis writer is careful to point out the magnanimity of Abram in comparison with Lot's greed. Eventually, however, God does not forsake Lot and his family since he obeyed God's word, even though reluctantly and with little faith (Gen. 19:1-15).

The compromise suggested by Abram is *not* a questionable one. The burden lay upon Lot and what he did with his opportunity. There is no indication at all that Lot and his family shared in the wickedness of Sodom. By living there, however, they showed a tolerance to evil which may have had an effect upon Lot's wife in her disobedience and the actions later of Lot's two daughters (Gen. 19:30-38). Lot was a middle-of-the roader.

To take a middle of the road position suggests to many people not a compromiser or a fence-straddler, but a person who is moderate and fair in thought and action.

He is not an extremist. He may be like the judge who wants to be just and is unwilling categorically to condemn others and come to a premature judgment before looking at every side of an issue.

Life's practical situations often present a predicament; but the Word of God gives us always excellent guidelines to aid us in decisions.

Paul is careful to cut back through century after century to the time of Moses in order to establish the gracious action of God from the beginning.

* * * * *

Is compromise always bad or are there occasions when it is justified?

How can we be certain that we are doing the right thing in decisions we make?

What are some guidelines for the Christian?

2nd Day — Lay It To Heart

I Corinthians 10:6-13

Scoffing at moral truths has become very common in our day. Examples from the past of those who have thought of themselves more highly than they ought to think (Rom. 12:3) and have fallen no longer seem to deter either the young or the old.

Of all the arguments that are given to prompt people not to take stands against evil, the most cogent is the one which stresses an ancient formula — *cultivate the golden mean.*

This means moderation. Such a man is one who steers his course by the rule that safety lies in the middle of the road. The format is a very familiar one, made up of well-worn cautions: first, no extremes or excesses; second, try not to be too much affected by the passion of the world; third, do not allow yourself to be hurt by standing too strongly on one side or the other.

There is an interesting and very significant point here that one ought to consider in terms of his own devotional life and daily responses to the situations which come to us all for decisions.

It is this - Jesus never compromised!

Sometimes he evaded direct confrontation, as when he perceived the people would come and take Him by force to make Him a king, "Jesus withdrew again to the hills by Himself (John 6:15)."

This of course is the reason the apostle Paul so strongly reminded the Corinthians of the examples of those who sinned. Do as Jesus did in your own life, be alone with God.

The forward march of the church was once affected by the view of *the golden mean.* It was a view held by Gamaliel, a member of the Sanhedrin, who advised moderation. Peter and John were brought before the Sanhedrin after Pentecost. Some wanted to kill them, but they listened to Gamaliel (Acts 5:38-39). Gamaliel may even have been partially persuaded by the work of the apostles.

* * * * *

Some might call Gamaliel's advice one of compromise. What do you think and why?

What are the proper distinctions between common sense and compromising with evil?

What are some personal examples of how you might be ready to fall when you think you are in control?

3rd Day — Altars for Sinning

I Corinthians 10:14-22

Even our approach to worship may create the possibility for compromising. Nothing escapes Paul's attention in making important distinctions.

For example, Paul tells the Corinthians to flee from idolatry (I Cor. 10:14). The Gentiles sacrifice to devils. Do not fellowship with devils (10:20). There are altars enough for sinning in life without creating additional ones.

Avoid compromising at all. We ought, however, to be willing to hear the arguments for walking in the middle of the road. How else can be understood the ramifications of compromise? How can we protect ourselves if we are unwilling to learn? That is to say, because we know what the arguments are for a compromising position, we need not follow them. But by knowing them, we will come to know why we do not do them - thus be aided.

The main values that have traditionally been given for moderation and the middle of the road, step by step, are quite convincing. One, it keeps us from emotional excesses of the religious impulse. Two, it recognizes intellect but prevents the logic of the intellect from going to excess.

Three, it provides a just basis for dealing with the difficulties and problems of life. Justice, it would be argued, is assured. Nothing is ever black or white in the moral realm.

Four, it gives men protection from the unnecessary hurts of life. It would be against the view that it is better to have loved and lost than never to have loved at all. It would advise, "Do not be hurt."

Some would even point to Scriptural evidence for moderation in all things, Ecclesiastes 7:16-17, not to be righteous overmuch or overmuch wicked.

There seem to be no sensible arguments to support the view that the writer of Ecclesiastes stands for compromise with evil. He believes in judgment (12:14).

*   *   *   *   *

In your own observations, what has happened to belief in the value of the Ten Commandments?

What are some of the arguments, other than above, for traveling the middle of the road?

What arguments can you muster against them?

4th Day — Dismayed For A Moment

I Corinthians 10:14-22

Here Paul makes a series of important distinctions which ought affect the actions of the Christian dealing with others. Read them carefully.

For example, there are many things you can do, that are lawful to do, that you ought not always do. Why ask questions to create difficulties over somebody else's scruples (I Cor. 10:23-24)?

The entire issue of what you should do instead of following someone else is crucial. Walk by day, not by night, in your thinking since it is better to see than to stumble (John 11:9-10). Our slight affliction is but for a moment (II Cor. 4:17), so do not be dismayed at a temporary pause which may come about because of another's influences.

In the long run, it is better to follow our own educated conscience, that is, one guided constantly by Christ, than to follow the uneducated conscience of another.

There are times, however we may be wise to follow the educated consciences of others: parents, teachers, or pastors. Sometimes in addition to the guidance of the Scriptures, lessons from history can become valuable guides.

John Wesley's revival in Great Britain in the 18th century brought forth a mountain of abuse from his opponents, mainly Anglican clergy who criticized his revival for what they termed its emotional excesses and its disruption of normal church life.

Yet, historians claim that the Wesleyan revival saved Great Britain from the excesses of the French Revolution by redirecting the moral energies of the people of that land.

There was also a Norwegian lay evangelist some years later than Wesley who was criticized in the same way. In Norway the end of the 18th century the clergy came up with several interesting sermon themes. Easter suggested, "The Value of Early Rising," and practical concerns brought out, "How to Grow Potatoes."

* * * * *

The values of good companions are very clear, but why should we not follow everything they *do?*

Why are disappointments sometimes more helpful than hindrances?

How might lessons from history open up new understanding of the Scriptures?

5th Day — Going Backward

Revelation 3:15-16

Some argue for adjustment of the church to society so the church does not get too far ahead of its people. They would then pause to understand, negotiate and reason such people into proper religious education.

That is what the church in Laodicea did. Certainly, it was a lukewarm church (Rev. 3:16) marching backward at a rapid pace.

The Norwegian lay evangelist referred to earlier was named Hans Nielsen Hauge. He made a valuable contribution to understanding the entire issue of compromising with evil. He also vigorously attacked the backward-going view of the spiritual life.

Hauge wrote to his people in response to his critics in the Norwegian Church: "Where does this middle way lead? For it is foolish to follow a road one does not know where it goes . . . In temporal things there may be a middle way. But if any one takes a middle way in spiritual things, then I do not doubt it runs along the broad road to hell."

Hauge reflected, of course, Jesus' admonition against following the broad way and Jesus' urging to enter the narrow gate because it leads to life but few find it (Mt. 7:13-14).

There are two things which should be said at this point about the influences exercised both by pastors and by spirit-filled lay people.

The first thing to recognize is that those who wish to be so understanding of the world have a completely false knowledge of the purpose of the church and the followers of Christ in the world.

The second thing is to look outward to see that we are not following the ways of other men, and also inward to judge our own motives.

The Christian and the church are both under orders not to be conformed to this world but to be transformed by renewed minds to prove the will of God and what is right (Rom. 12:2).

* * * * *

For your own growth, no matter what your own position, criticize the approach to church life you like best.

Now defend the approach to church life you like least.

What has been the value of this exercise?

6th Day — The Everlasting Yea

II Corinthians 1:15-22

Do not be of a doubtful mind (Lk. 12:2), but be positive of your stand toward God. Say, "Yes" constantly to God. Do not be doubleminded and unstable (James 1:8).

The sweet reasonableness of the middle of the road, the persuasiveness of the world, and even the compromising attitudes of many leaders in the churches today cannot ever hide the basic flaws against playing loose with God's ways.

Consider the defects of an attitude which stresses the middle of the road. One, compromise is invited and encouraged even if matters are fairly clearcut. If it has worked to an advantage once why not again, and again, and again. Our day has witnessed a great deal of this.

Two, the middle of the road leads to indifference to valid criticisms. If everything always is blurred, then why listen to criticisms at all. None can really be valid. This leads to much blundering.

Three, the delays of the middle of the road encourage the wicked. They have gotten away with it once, why not again. There are always those who stand to be rewarded by delays. People forget, get tired, and are unwilling to persevere. Life is too short.

Four, the middle of the road gives no direction at all to main issues of life: suffering, injustices, pain, birth, life, and death.

In life we do not deal with reasonableness, according to man's standards, and with light and easy issues. If we could, for example, always be contemplative and take all the time we need to be orderly in everything, there might - just might - be some justification for the middle of the road as a way of life.

But death comes swiftly. Losses come unexpectedly. In the twinkling of an eye we stand before a changed set of circumstances and need to decide *now,* not tomorrow.

* * * * *

Suppose you were able to take all the time in the world to some problems you face now, do you think the choices would be any easier?

What additional arguments can you give against the middle of the road as a way of life?

7th Day — With Terrifying Power

II Peter 2:4-10

Read the lessons of the past as Peter describes them. God has two powers - one terrifying and one gracious, and there is no question but that his gracious power is always extended.

But forget not God's terrifying power. God's love is everlasting, but He hates evil. If the fate of Jesus, a good man, is crucifixion, what will be the fate of those who do not have His goodness (Lk. 23:31)?

We stand in a new world, a new age. To Jesus Christ as our Saviour we must be fully committed. There can be no middle of the road religiously.

In temporal questions, where moot issues are concerned, there is a way out where one may differ with another. But in all things, the disciple of Christ, whether toward another disciple or a non-believer, must have a spirit of generosity and understanding.

Jesus certainly recognized distinctions between the temporal and the spiritual realm when the Pharisees, on this very issue, attempted to entangle him in his talk. In response to the question of tribute money, Jesus answered, "Render therefore to Caesar the things that are Caesar's, and to God the things that are God's (Mt. 22:15-21)."

Spiritually, there can be no middle way. The Christian is one who risks everything for the love of Christ. For Christ the believer will not budge. He will stand firm and will withstand the coaxings of evil (Eph. 6:13-14).

On this essential matter, for all Christians, there should be basic unity.

The cause of the church all over the world has suffered because of confusion between the temporal and the spiritual area.

In your life you ought carefully consider the distinctions made here, recognizing that each of us is a pilgrim - a stranger and exile - on this earth (Heb. 11:13), not a permanent resident.

* * * * *

What is the function of the pilgrim?
What are the characteristics and attitudes of a pilgrim?
Our earth is a home, but why then should we be called "strangers"?

What is a Christian Church? The answer must be given: "A large family under God. The Church should unlock doors, open hearts and minds, clear cobwebs of traditionalism for its own sake, and open vistas of mountains to climb and deserts to cross."

The Church should call its whole family, under God, into wholeness. It is not only that Christians should get set for a great adventure - as though it were totally future - but know they are in the adventure even now.

You and all other believers make up Christ's Church in the midst of the battle but not in the middle of the road!

ECCLESIASTES 3

16 Moreover I saw under the sun that
in the place of justice, even there was wickedness, and in the place of righteousness,
even there was wickedness.

THE TENTH WEEK
MORE THAN CONQUERORS

Introductory Bible reading for this week:
Romans 12:14-21

Actions very often come before the wording of the principle that may be involved. In addition one must take into account what a man believes and how strongly he believes it.

Isaac had every reason to make war and not have peace, from a human standpoint, with Abimelech and the Philistines. They became jealous of his wealth and the wells he had. The Philistines stopped the wells, and filled them with earth (Gen. 26).

However, Isaac moved on, digged again the wells of water his father Abraham had digged. They still quarreled with him, so Isaac moved again.

Paul years later formulated what Isaac had practiced: "If possible, so far as it depends upon you, live peaceably with all (Rom. 12:18)."

1st Day — From God's Mouth

Genesis 26:1-5

Do you *dare* to change?

Everyone fears change and resists it. If you should say, "This is not true. I would like to change from what I am to what I could be," it would have to be pointed out that the desire to change is not the same as changing. Conflicts result from obstinacy.

You may desire change with all your heart, but when opportunities to change come to each of us, we will first resist it. There would be fear of change.

The tendency to remain what we are is greater than the tendency to change. A body in motion tends to remain in motion. A body at rest tends to remain at rest. You will recognize the simple law in physics. The law may be applied to human behavior.

The eye tends to reject a contact lens. The mouth tends to reject a bridge. What *is* tends to be stronger than what *might* or could be.

God knows all this, so He enters into human history in events both in the lives of persons and of nations. The Lord appeared to Isaac, spoke to him, and made a covenant or agreement with him (Gen. 26:2-5). Isaac's heart was changed, and then he acted out of what had come from God's mouth: over and over again, from the beginning, "And God said (Gen. 1:3)," and something happened.

To change, therefore, to arrest a body in motion, to move a body at rest, to have the eye accept a contact lens or the mouth a bridge all require a new and more powerful force than the one which exists.

The principle is true whether one deals with habits, attitudes, behavior patterns, or material objects. The obstacle remains unless a powerful force uproots it. The boulder stays unless a bulldozer moves it.

Tensions, conflicts - they follow the same path. They will continue to exist *unless* the power of God through Jesus Christ forces a personal revolution.

* * * * *

What are ways that you would like to change but keep finding excuses not to do so?

How can you find this power, or this force, to push to make the decision to create what you want?

Can you understand why the word "dare" is used in the question? Does it not take daring to change?

2nd Day — A Deadly Arrow

James 4:1-3

The apostle Paul was a good man. He was a follower of the law and zealous in striking back, before his conversion, at Christians who he believed perverted the law.

However, within Paul at one time was a deadly arrow of destruction, a warring among his own members and the same lust of the flesh of which James writes (Rom. 7:7-23).

Who then could speak with greater authority than Paul concerning a thorough-going change from what was old to that which was new? Now if Paul who was good according to the standards of his own people regarded himself as worse than nothing and unable to be set right before God except through Jesus Christ, then all must recognize the problem. The problem? The deadly arrow of destruction within each one of us. We cannot do the good we want, and the evil we do not want is what we do (Rom. 7:19).

Paul had been adamant in his opposition to the Christian Way. On the Damascus Road he was given the power to change.

The change was dramatic and immediate, but the struggle had been going on for many years. God had been operating in Paul's life, but he was going in the wrong direction.

In one instance, then, after long struggle, Paul was given the means whereby he could change. He accepted Christ. God then through Christ continued to be active in his life to accomplish a constant renewing and revolutionary adjustment.

Each one of us needs the knowledge of this experience. The deadly arrow of lust or inordinate desire for anything and division in self must be destroyed. The question, Dare I change? must be answered affirmatively. Renewing the spirit of one's mind to put on the new man (Eph. 4:23-24) is the first step toward a way of peace in self and with others.

* * * * *

What values are treaties or agreements without inner assent?

Can you think of other passages of Scripture which illumine the way to change or to peace?

What are they? Look them up and digest them.

3rd Day — Contention and Agreement

Genesis 26:17-22, 26-31

Consider what might result if you, as Christ's disciple, increased your pace just slightly: one more prayer and reading one more verse of Scripture daily. When our pace is slow, it shows that our belief is weak.

The point is that God teaches all men. God can teach you, and no man need fear his lack of formal education in matters of faith. Wisdom from God does not come from classrooms and books, especially when it comes to conflict situations. One can observe this truth.

Striving or contending seems to be built into many of life's situations. Isaac faced that with the herdsmen of Gerar (Gen. 26:20), but Isaac did one thing more. He refused to fight over what had other solutions. God sustained and directed Isaac, assuring him of the future (Gen. 26:24).

However, Isaac did not hesitate honestly to confront Abimilech, his friend, and one of his captains and ask them bluntly why they had come and why they hated him (Gen. 26:27).

Isaac's openness led to an agreement (Gen. 26:28-29) between them because they saw in Isaac that the Lord was with him (Gen. 26:28).

A vision is needed for one to act as Isaac did. It may be small, like the streak of sunshine that entered our sick room when as a child we were ill. Or, like the first penny we ever earned.

The size of the vision matters little. It need not be dramatic. God was with Isaac in his normal working day.

The vision need only hold out hope of the possibility of power that is greater than the power which holds us down or back. To desire to change a single habit or your entire way of life requires a dream, a hope, or a vision.

It also works in reverse. A bad habit or a sinful way of life begins by a vision or a dream of temptation. Not all at once, but gradually decision by decision the wrong attitudes get established and control us.

* * * * *

Do you think that Isaac's backing away indicated that he wanted peace at any price? Why?

Can you name some things worth dying for other than country or for one's family?

Are there any?

The next time you are in a conflict situation, try one more prayer and one more verse of Scripture.

4th Day — Strong Hands

Romans 12:9-13

These verses of Paul to the Romans further extend the possibilities of other steps a Christian must take to do his duty. They are not easy. They cannot be done with one's own strength.

The way out of an evil life, or even a life not noted either for great goodness or for great sinning, is still a series of small steps, small decisions, one by one, stemming from the small vision of what God puts in one's heart.

There is nothing complimentary in the usual meaning attached to the comment, "My, he is only a shadow of his former self." Or, to put it another way, "He is not the man he used to be."

The observation may be made in shocked surprise, after seeing an old friend or acquaintance for the first time in many years: "How distressing it was to see him!"

Sadness may be expressed. "When you think of what he once was! Or, is it not a shame that he has fallen on such evil days!"

Even sadder, of course, is the deterioration which takes place within a person which cannot be outwardly observed.

From the thinking of the apostle Paul, spiritually speaking, the statement that you are only a shadow of your former self might be a compliment and may be expressed with joy.

Is it not wonderful that he is only a shadow of what he formerly used to be?

Paul does not want a man or a woman to be what he was. The assumption here is that Christians must clearly be different from what they were. Old things, the former life, must pass away.

Be renewed in the spirit of your mind (Eph. 4:23). Change. It is not so much, when we come to think of it, to accept our duty and our loving obedience. Love needs to be open.

God needs the strong hands of all Christians.

* * * * *

Begin to list the habits you have, the ones you like and the ones you do not like. What to do?

Now what is your vision, how would you describe it to help you do something about your habits?

What can you do then to follow them always?

5th Day — Skilled Dealings

Romans 12:14-21

Paul reiterates our Lord's teachings when he tells the Romans to bless those who persecute you. Feed your enemy. Give him water to drink. Heap coals of fire on his head - that is to say, as usually interpreted, make the enemy feel ashamed by meeting his evil with good (Prov. 25:21-22).

There is a higher purpose in this, however, than to shame your enemy. It is this: do what you have committed yourself to do as a Christian so you do not need to be *ashamed of yourself.*

This interpretation is verified by Paul's saying, "If it be possible, so far as it depends on you, live peaceably with all (Rom. 12:18)."

You owe it to yourself. You owe it to God. Do not be the one to provoke enmity. If you discover you are the provoker, stop. Stop being the irritant.

It is in the area of dealing with enmity, with one's enemies, with those who anger or provoke us, that the Christian needs the greatest of skill.

One can love foolishly. One can compromise in a dangerous manner. It is indeed difficult to resist the ways of the world lovingly.

The devil tempted Jesus in the wilderness. Jesus said, "Begone, Satan (Mt. 4:10)!" This was a decisive act. It is as though Jesus said, "Once for all, I cut you off, Satan, abruptly, without doubt, with faith that I must follow and worship God only and serve only Him."

That is the beginning of skilled dealings with evil. In an instant, be done with it, make the decision. An evil companion may have to be cut off, but that is only the beginning.

Three times Jesus had to cut off the devil in the wilderness. Perhaps one may need three times thirty, but it must be done.

The skill involves first making *one decision* - which side are you going to be on, God's or Satan's? Many Christians keep fluctuating. They never choose.

* * * * *

What should your response be when enmity is continued or provoked in spite of what you do?

Jesus castigated the Pharisees and the Sadducees, but he also wept over Jerusalem. What does this indicate about Jesus?

Is every conflict worthless? Why or why not?

6th Day — Lengthen Your Cords

Romans 13:1-10

Paul writes in summation of the above passage: "Love does no wrong to a neighbor; therefore love is the fulfilling of the law (Rom. 13:10)."

As with so many of the important Christian precepts, one must broaden, deepen, and lengthen one's normal understandings. For example, Paul teaches us to follow the law of the state. He writes that the powers that be are ordained of God (Rom. 13:1). Yet, Peter and John clearly indicate to the high priest and others that they must obey God rather than the laws of man (Acts 4:19).

Some have regarded these positions as contradictory. They are not. They are rather two sides of the same coin. The law of the land may have to be changed, but obedience to it is necessary unless for conscience's sake it is impossible.

Christians must let their wisdom bear upon the problems of our generation in this regard, siding neither with the lawless nor the rigid legalists until careful determination can be made of the issues at stake.

If law is the outgrowth of love - as it clearly is in the Scriptures - then both law and love play important roles in the life of man.

The need, then, is to think more biblically. We cannot think biblically until we know the Bible.

True prayer may lead us to the Bible. There we can read, when we wonder about the difficulties of life and the temptations of it that God will not let us be tempted beyond our capacity (1 Cor. 10:13).

The temptation may exist not to see both sides of the coin of love and law. Maudlin love may be easier to follow. Law for law's sake is a simpler way out than thinking and making decisions.

Note for yourself over and over again how Jesus *thought about problems.* He was not just clever; he was intelligent about them. When you are tempted to give quick and facile answers, think! Christ did.

* * * * *

What are some of the other tensions which exist in Christian ways of living? Discuss with someone else these apparently contradictory aspects of love and law.

Then share these thoughts with another.

7th Day — When There Is No Peace

I Peter 3:8-18

Evil persons are the most consistent people in the world. The intelligent Christian, on the other hand, is wise enough to be inconsistent.

Consider the passage in I Peter, where the advice is given to Christians to act contrariwise to those who would do us harm (I Pet. 3:9). Yet on and on evil persons persist on their evildoings. Consistently they pursue their activity.

Intelligent Christians by their actions, though all the evil in the world be against them, respond with love, a response abnormal to the ways of the world. Therefore, they are being inconsistent to the ways of the world.

Yet the world and evil persons within it keep on working their ways against God.

Great value is placed humanly on consistency. Men fear to be called fickle. Never contradict yourself. Lie and then lie again to cover up the first lie. Be consistent. Pride is back of this view.

One who honestly seeks God's will daily is bound to be inconsistent. When greater experience or knowledge come the old will be relinquished for the new. God's truth is always the same, certain and true, steadfast and immoveable.

But the changes that take place in Christians as they grow is in them, not in the truth that God has given the world.

Men try to trade places with God, as all dictators do. They are absolutely consistent with their system. Leaving God out, they can kill without mercy.

One has to admit that the way of the Pharisees as described in the Gospels is a description of one of the world's greatest consistent religious systems.

A puzzled Pharisee once came to Jesus, Nicodemus (John 3). When Jesus said he must be born again (John 3:3), Nicodemus' problem was that he could not think inconsistently. Man's way is not God's (I Sam. 16:7).

* * * * *

How might peace be achieved in your life and in the world by being inconsistent?

What are some biblical examples other than have been mentioned that show ways inconsistent with the world?

Why are you afraid sometimes to change your mind?

Man's consistency is the enemy of change and of peace in the world. Spontaneity and creative living liven the joys of Christian living.

Your mind wants to go in one direction. God says to go in another. So the Christian must contradict himself, he must be inconsistent with what he really is in order to follow God's will.

Growing is not easy. Growth demands something of us. God's Word never leaves us alone, when we understand it and are willing to follow it. It disturbs us. A mind keen and alert, eager for guidance, and tough for the battle of life is what should be sought.

PSALM 138

[7] Though I walk in the midst of trouble,
thou dost preserve my life,

THE ELEVENTH WEEK
RUN THE STRAIGHT RACE

**Introductory Bible reading for this week:
I John 2:12-17**

Most of us need to be reminded that the old and familiar farewell "good-bye" means "God be with you." Today's favorite farewell is no longer "God be with you," but *take it easy.*

Calm down, relax, do not try to set the world on fire. Americans have been taking it easy for many generations and the results have been undermining personal and national character.

Crookedness now has become normal. Take it easy. Cut a corner here and there. Do not be so conscientious.

However, the problem seems to be as old as man. Esau gave away his birthright for a mess of pottage (Gen. 25:30-34). The danger always is present that each generation may sell out to the world.

1st Day — A Troubled Sea

Hebrews 12:12-17

Why would Esau sell his birthright for one morsel of meat (Heb.12:16)? The birthright according to Jewish law (Dt. 21:15-17) made the eldest son the head of the family and gave him the largest share of the property.

The answer must be that Esau loved immediate satisfaction of his appetites more than the higher values of his birthright.

Esau looked not to the future but to the moment.

To submit to fleshly appetites is to deny the spirit and to ignore the promises of the future. As Paul writes, those who are led by the Spirit of God are the sons of God and the sufferings of the present are not worthy to be compared with the glory which will be revealed to us (Rom. 8:14,18).

It was not so with Esau. The intemperance of the immediate present meant far more to him than the temperance of the future.

It is for this reason that the New Testament classifies Esau as "profane (Heb. 12:16)." In Jesus' teachings Esau exalted the fleshly appetites and was humbled (Lk. 18:14).

The Gospel of Jesus Christ does strike many negative notes, all with the purpose of awakening people to more basic personal needs. "Repent," Jesus said when he came into Galilee, preaching the gospel of the kingdom of God, "and believe in the gospel (Mk. 1:14-15)."

Repentance is humbling, but there is the gospel, "good news."

Repentance is the stairway we must climb, through peril, toil, and pain - personal and national - to come to know the amazing love, the irrestible grace of God in order to believe the eternally positive good news of Jesus Christ.

It seems very evident that man today is quite clever, or so he thinks. Yet, all is not well. Fear rules like a troubled sea our secular society.

* * * * *

In what ways can we say Esau was immoral and irreligious?
To whom, or to what kind of persons could Esau be likened today?
Are we then judging Esau to criticize him?

2nd Day — Cry In the Wilderness

I John 2:12-17

The words of John in this letter are like a cry in the wilderness. They are words that are not heard today. If they should be heard in the cities, they would be laughed at: "Do not love the world or the things in the world (I Jn. 2:15)."

At this point you ought to ask yourself whether the things in the world are evil or wicked *in themselves.* Of course they are not. God looked at His creation and saw that it was good (Gen. 1:31). Yet, does this mean that there is a contradiction here? No, it does not. How is this so?

It is not the things of the world which are in themselves wicked but in giving up our will to them, in allowing them to control us. The food that Esau ate was not in itself bad. What was wrong was in Esau, his intemperance. God does not create us automatically geared to do His will. Our response is our own. It is free.

Consider our society in its *secularism,* a word which means "pertaining to the worldly or temporal," - secularism: *the new religion of our day!* That is to say, being secular in outlook is to make a God of the belly and mind only earthly things (Phil. 3:19).

The end of such things is destruction. Moral and social problems today have become uncontrollable monsters. Knowledge of science clearly outstrips our capacity to control the results.

Our national ability to produce exciting, even if sometimes deceitful, TV commercials is far ahead of our capacity to produce realistic solutions to our personal, social, educational, and international problems.

Large areas of the churches are also controlled by secular attitudes. The response among Christians has not been conducive to confidence in the Christian way of life: angry shouting and deliberate division; or equating success — being a good salesman — with being Christian.

The only positive thing which can be said is that out of this confusion of what Christianity is may rise awareness of what is necessary to put the Christian house in order.

* * * * *

In what ways can you contribute to the turning from secularism to the Christian way of life?

From your own work experience, or at home, how would you illustrate today's threats?

How strong a "religion" do you believe secularism has become?

3rd Day — Hail To The Sun Returning

I John 2:7-11

Hatred destroys both the possibility of realistic solutions to problems and the person who hates. One ought never forget that God is ever present even in the darkness of secularism. He is ready to open hearts to see the light which already is shining. When darkness covers the sun on a day that means so much for the family on an outing, how thrilling it is to have the sun return.

Now we can count on the fact that God does not forsake us ever. However, our turning is necessary to see the light he sheds in the darkness.

Some years ago Americans could have been criticized as being like the Pharisee (Lk. 18:11-12): believing in self, having a good opinion of self compared to others, or a corporate American spiritual pride.

However, today our pride has slipped. We no longer are sure of ourselves. We are now living in the atmosphere which follows the result of having once been Pharisaical. We are disillusioned Pharisees.

We once had exalted ourselves and are now being humbled. Ours is a genuine dilemma.

We who trusted only in ourselves, our strength, and our ability to produce and our capacity to solve problems quickly and forthrightly now face problems where the old solutions do not work.

The old individualism and the old cock-of-the-walk methods have failed. Yet we cling to them because we know no other ways.

Our corporate and individual spiritual pride of the past have trapped us. We have not yet found the way out.

An individual, just as the nation, may still stir in the embers of old fires, but they will not rekindle.

This personal and corporate dilemma, when the old methods are used, is like a man sitting down to write an unbiased account of the Civil War from the southern point of view. Obviously, the result will mean nothing.

*   *   *   *   *

Has the world grown beyond Christians, and are we the ones who need to catch up?

Are we standing still in a day of change?

Do we act like sensitive Christians seeking not our will but God's in every new situation?

4th Day — Double Trouble

Romans 9:1-5

Paul writes of "great sorrow and unceasing anguish in my heart (Rom. 9:2)" because he sees unbelief continuing among his own people, the Israelites.

One must follow Paul's argument carefully and note that he wishes he could take the punishment for his people for their not seeing the promises of God.

Clinging to the old ways is very natural. Only occasionally is the truth revealed. A Scandinavian clergyman once told of the many committees which had been formed to study the various spiritual and moral problems of the land.

They gathered all the facts, analyzed the problems, and came up with what appeared to be a reasonable solution.

"Then," the Scandinavian clergyman sadly observed, "we discovered that we had taken so long to analyze the problems by the time we got around to them the problems had changed."

So the problem unresolved because of delay and slow methods, had added a new dimension, which might be called *double trouble*.

Delays are damaging and destructive. Paul's people, as the prophets had discovered before him, were just like other people - they dragged their heels. The evidence before them they refused to see.

Or, if they saw it, they refused to move quickly enough toward solution. Delay only compounds the difficulties.

This ought to be a lesson for the individual Christian. Every day you let go by making promises you do not keep, you heap up *double trouble*.

Repentance is the only way out. Repentance is an offense to our spiritual pride. We want to think highly of ourselves. My, how happy we are that we are not like other men (Lk. 18:11)!

The American form of secularism has given rise to a greater flowering of this ancient heresy of man's goodness. So there is a greater need.

* * * * *

What examples can you give from your own religious experience to show how delays lead to trouble?

Note how Paul's concern for his people did not lead him to forsake going on himself. How might you apply this to someone you know?

How is repentance not degrading but positive?

5th Day — Men and Women of Promise

Romans 9:6-13

The cry of Joel seems particularly relevant to our day in its need to make up its mind whether to follow God or continue in the threat of secularism: "Multitudes, multitudes in the valley of decision! For the day of the Lord is near in the valley of decision (Joel 3:14)."

Repentance at times seems outmoded by modern insights about human nature, but this is in appearance only. Notice how the problems get worse rather than better, even though it appears people know or say they know more today about what makes people respond in proper ways. What do they know? Does what they know solve crucial problems?

The ancient words of the Scriptures about confession of sins stand as eternally significant and deep words, describing accurately the human situation, in a world of shifting values. They call us each time we say them to striking hard blows for real freedom and for the dignity of man.

Confession of one's sins is not degrading or pessimistic. It rather is enlivening.

We are still men and women of promise, living under the same rule of God applicable for Abraham and Sarah and Jacob and Esau (Rom. 9:7-9). Furthermore, God loves men and women of the promise of faith and hates those who live by flesh, as with Jacob and Esau (Rom. 9:13).

Yet, "hate" in this sense is not the hatred of men. God loves all His creation. He broods over His world, seeking to give His salvation. He woos men and women with His love.

Confess your sins then. When you do acknowledge them, the dilemma of your life and the dilemma of American national life will crack wide open. There will come vistas of meaning and direction spread before all people like the fields of bluebonnets in the spring of the Texas countryside.

Repentance leads to humbleness. To walk humbly before God will lead to true exaltation.

* * * * *

How does the Lord's Prayer present the matter of confession of sins? Note the connection between the need for our forgiveness and ours of others.
What are the ways that God might hate and love at the same time?
What does it mean to be men and women of promise?

118

6th Day — A Great Conflict

Romans 13:11-14

Christians have a major responsibility and duty to take part in reversing the trends to *take it easy.* This is still a great nation, but the fires of faith need to be rekindled. We cannot continue to live on the ashes of the fires of the past.

The nature of the problem of secularism is that secularism is pitted against God and God's people. It is essential that we wake out of sleep (Rom. 13:11) and get ready for battle (Rom. 13:12).

The Christian ought to live in that light. Hostility ranged against Christians. Warfare of evil against goodness.

If everyone could be misled into believing that there is no hostility, that there is no warfare, and that *take it easy* is a good philosophy, this is ideal for secularism. If *take it easy* - the desire not to get involved, to seek one's own security primarily, to shrink from the battle, even closing one's eyes to its existence - can become the guiding rule of all Christians then they can be won without a clash of physical force. They then will simply succumb to the opposition by their blandishments of ease.

Christians must lead. The battle is real. Consider the words of an old hymn:

> Christian, dost thou see them
> On the holy ground,
> How the powers of darkness
> Rage thy steps around?
> Christian dost thou feel them,
> How they work within,
> Striving, tempting, luring,
> Goading into sin?

Suppose you do not recognize the hostility. Suppose you give just a little ground. Add your life now to millions, conflict after conflict, a slip here, a slip there, little by little, little by little. A great avalanche is the result.

There are many who say that an avalanche of wickedness cannot be stopped. Do not believe it. Fight, with God.

* * * * *

What special problems face the Christian in a society where there is great abundance?

Is it necessary for the Christian to live as though there were hostility all around?

What hope is there for victory?

7th Day — Bearing With the Weak

Romans 14:1-54

What an unusal fighter the Christian is! He has understanding for the weak (Rom. 14:1) in the faith. The ways of the world are clearly different.

"We have unmistakable proof," writes Herbert Spencer in his *First Principles,* "that throughout all past time, there has been a ceaseless devouring of the weak by the strong."

The observation is certainly correct. Yet this does not allow us the pride to believe that because Christians are to bear with the weak *they do as Paul advises.* The contrary, just as in the world, unfortunately has often been true of Christians. Look into congregational life. Look into family life.

What do you observe? What have you known to be true about yourself?

Now, this should not be misunderstood, this asking of questions. It has the purpose only of encouraging complete and thorough honesty in all relationships with others.

When Judas Iscariot thought he had an advantage over Jesus, he used it to his own guilt and loss. Examine the Pauline letters of the New Testament and note how when Paul appears to be weak, many in the congregations he had founded worked against him.

Therefore, it is not only the world the Christian needs to fear. He needs to fear, first, his own reactions when he is strong. He needs, second, to know that Christians will hurt sometimes, unfortunately, other Christians *if* they think they can get away with it. The reasons are puzzling, sometimes quite obscure, but observation shows that it is nevertheless true.

Often Christians act as though God is dead and that this world is like a railroad train roaring through space with the engineer lying dead on the engine floor.

Reject, therefore the philosophy *take it easy.* There is no rest for the Christian. The sooner this is accepted as true, the closer the Kingdom.

* * * * *

How can you help restore one member of the church of Christ who has been hurt by other members?

Answer the question convincingly to an unbeliever: Who rules the world, God or the Devil?

How may differences even cement Christians?

Learn to accept the challenges of faith and move ahead. Tackle the unfulfilled goals. Dream the dreams still undreamed. Do this just when you have decided that you have done your best, and you can do no more. Take one more step, then another.

This world requires such men and women of God. All of this is not something we would do by our will. We do it by the power of the living God in Christ Jesus.

By our refusing to accept the philosophy of *take it easy* in the weeks and months to come we will be astonished beyond measure at our progress in faith. In addition, we will be pleased to see changes in others as well as in ourselves.

HEBREWS 12

12 Therefore lift your drooping hands and strengthen your weak knees, 13 and make straight paths for your feet, so that what is lame may not be put out of joint but rather be healed.

THE TWELFTH WEEK
BELONGING TO THE WAY

Introductory Bible reading for this week:
John 1:43-51

"You shall see greater things than these," Jesus said to Nathaniel because of his belief in Him (John 1:50). This is certainly true, though some doubt.

From the days of the Apostles until the Emperor Constantine's edict of toleration in 313 A.D., Christian disciples lived under the threat of death.

"Day by day we are besieged; day by day we are betrayed," said Tertullian, one of the most gifted and remarkable personalities of the ancient church, "oftentimes in the very midst of our meetings and gatherings, we are surprised by assault."

Yet, the second century Christians refused to absent themselves from their worship. For them there was a compelling urgency towards corporate worship which came out of the very nature of the Christian faith.

Note the thread of spiritual pilgrimage in the Scriptures.

1st Day — Awakened Hearts

2 Corinthians 3:1-6

It was not the law of Abraham and Isaac which changed Jacob from a deceiver to a man of God - it was the presence of God in Jacob's life (Gen: 27:16) and his struggling with God (Gen. 32:24-30). It has always been this way. It can be the same with you.

The presence of God seems most to be understood as a vision, a strong emotion, or the power of the Spirit of God moving within. But, struggle? How can this struggle be so important?

It happens as follows. A man or a woman may feel right with God. They sense, or know, they have been saved. Yet, except for this inward knowledge not a great deal happens in their lives different from other years.

John Wesley used to say that unless a believer knew for certain he had been saved and has assurance of it, he had not been saved.

As the years went by and the revival of the 18th century in Great Britain grew in strength Wesley revised his view about assurance. He did so because he observed that there were many whose lives were exemplary as followers of Christ who worried about their lack of assurance because they did not have a conscious awareness of salvation.

Why worry consciences needlessly? Wesley reasoned, especially when he also observed that some who were most certain of the assurance of their salvation did not always show it by changed lives.

Yet, struggle for the Christian, or a wrestling with the things of God versus the things of the world, is universal. Jacob's struggle took the form of wrestling with God. Isaiah saw the Lord high and lifted up (Is. 6:1-8) and immediately he felt himself to be a man of unclean lips.

Peter struggled in the courtyard and denied Christ three times (Lk. 22:61). Paul had his struggle on the Damascus Road (Acts 9:1-8). Christians still, today too, need to struggle.

Life is not easy for Christians *unless* their hearts are awakened by His presence and they struggle.

* * * * *

The similarities of religious experience between Old and New Testaments figures is clear. How?
How do these experiences differ?
Can you point to an experience, a time, a struggle in your life?
Why is this neglected in Christian thought?

2nd Day — The Lord's Freedom

2 Corinthians 3:12-18

In the Acts of the Apostles, Saul is described as trying to capture those *belonging to the Way (9:1-2)*.

Many would reason that it is easier today to belong to the 'Way,' as Christianity has been called, than in those early days. They were threatened. We are not threatened. They were surprised by assault. We are not surprised by assault.

Belonging to the Way is just as difficult now as then. There are always threats and assaults from the world, from other Christians, and from within. Sensitivity is required to be aware of genuine crises.

The Lord gives us freedom and power to belong to the Way, but we must turn to Him: "where the Spirit of the Lord is, there is freedom (2 Cor. 3:17)."

In the Galatian letter the apostle Paul treats the problem of Judaizers who advocated a rejection of Paul's teaching concerning the law and justification by faith.

Paul was a latecomer into the apostolic Church. Human nature in the middle of the first century was very much like it is now. In any controversy men do not hesitate to attack the character of their opponents to destroy their ideas.

Paul's apostolic authority rather than the issues was attacked.

First, Paul established his apostolic authority, the sum of his argument being that his authority comes from God not men (Gal. 1:12). But he also points out that he was given authority at the first council in Jerusalem in his own missionary work.

Even Peter he later rebukes and attacks for his dissimulation: "I opposed him to his face (Gal. 2:11)."

Paul realized, much as he knew of the values of the laws of the people of Israel and of lessons learned from men like Jacob, in love there was another way to handle problems, issues, and disagreements (2 Cor. 12-13): *plain speech*.

* * * * *

What is the Way of the World and how does it differ in the main from the Christian Way?

How can you continue to be a follower of the New Covenant and yet learn from the Old Testament? What lessons do you learn from Jacob?

3rd Day — Expect the Unexpected

2 Corinthians 5:1-5

There are times when we seem to think of the Holy Scriptures unrealistically. We think of them as not related to life. Certainly, knowing Paul's experiences with his churches, it must be admitted Paul speaks out of life. He pulled no ideas from the air.

He could not have made up the description of despair and affliction given to us when he groans to be in heaven and out of the body (2 Cor. 5:2).

Paul could treat the great themes of our faith precisely because he struggled to understand them. So it should be with us. They must be lived.

How unexpected the attack from Peter must have been when he denied the Jerusalem council's findings, and Paul had to strike back at him. How else did Paul come to know the dividing lines of his thought and the delineation of the meaning of his words?

Someone has to speak the opposite sometimes for us to react or to understand. So it must have been with Paul.

He learned, therefore, to live with the unexpected, evermore, *to expect the unexpected*. So out of the attack of the Galatian Judaizers and most certainly the personal presence and position of Peter, Paul enunciates the truth.

The great theme of Galatians comes to be freedom: "For freedom Christ has set us free; stand fast therefore, and do not submit again to a yoke of slavery (Gal. 5:1)." Christians are free to do all things.

Yet the freedom is not license. This is a paradox. It creates a tension. Learn to understand it. Expect the unexpected as a follower of the Way.

There are sometimes paradox and tension in the Gospel. You are free, yet you observe others' freedom as well. Jacob and Esau saw this principle (Gen. 33:10-11).

The Galatian letter stands as a constant warning to the church in all ages to know its theology of salvation. It rebukes selfishness. It projects a vision of a new man and a new woman in Christ.

* * * * *

What persons with whom you may have had a disagreement have taught you important lessons?
In Jesus' teaching where does he speak of expecting the unexpected?
What does this mean to you in your life?
What flexibility is required to be prepared?

4th Day — Faith-Action

2 Corinthians 5:6-10

The Christian has his eye on two worlds, one the present and the other the world which is to come. While he is present in this world, he walks by faith, not by sight (2 Cor. 5:7) and is willing not to neglect the life which is to come. Either way, the Christian aims to be accepted by God (2 Cor. 5:9).

Jacob worked in this world and while he did not have the hope of the Christian for the resurrection from the dead still he had a hope for the future.

It is not the same as the resurrection, but it is like it, and men at times will be moved to do things in the present for the hope that future generations will have standing. God's blessing and promise is of that type to Jacob in the Old Testament (Gen. 28: 13-15).

So Jacob was guided also in his hope for the future. Jacob had more than opinions about God. He had God's promises, but those promises had to wait many thousands of years before they reached the fulfillment of the full promises of the future life other than through one's children. Even non-believers have a kind of belief in the future through offspring.

Still, Jacob's belief was born of belief in the power of God to do as he had promised. This was the added dimension *over* non-believers.

Within the revelation of God at that point in history, the faith that Jacob had could still be termed faith-action. It was trust which led to living by its belief and trust.

Then it turns in the New Testament into greater faith-action because God shows love to man in his final way by giving up his Son to win the whole world.

There are many gifts but the greatest is love. This love is not sentimentality or pious agreement when none exists. This is what it means to belong to the Way. To be, think, and reconcile in love. Faith-action out of love.

* * * * *

Is it duty alone which prompts you to do what is necessary for those not of your family?

In fact, do you have any duty toward those outside of your family?

How do you produce action from faith?

5th Day — The Yoke of Christ

2 Corinthians 5:11-15

There is much in this passage which is a reminder of Jesus saying, "Take my yoke upon you, and learn from me; for I am gentle and lowly in heart, and you will find rest for your souls (Mt. 11:29)."

We do this, as Paul says, to persuade men (2 Cor. 5:11). Do we do it out of the terror of the Lord? Yes, one could say that. "Terror" here does not mean being thoroughly frightened. It is, rather, being completely and thoroughly aware of what is at stake, the judgment of the future.

It is not that the "terror," which may well be considered "fearful awe," of the judgment is to be our only or even chief motivation for good works or bearing Christ's yoke. It helps us to know truly how bracing and strenuous Paul's view of belonging to the Way was.

You cannot slide into heaven on your family's good works. You cannot, as so many individuals do, leave it to one particular member of the family to carry the load for you.

Paul is very clear on this: judgment will be given "so that each one may receive good or evil, according to what he has done in the body (II Cor. 5:10)."

In another place Paul puts it differently, but with the same end in mind: "For each man will have to bear his own load (Gal. 6:5)."

Jacob, even though he had been deceitful, would be judged according to how he had changed. Esau, even though he had been intemperate, would also be judged by his future trust in God.

This is more than opinion. Jesus had good opinions, but he had more. Jesus taught the truth. Anyone can have opinions. Not everyone can lay claim to having the truth. Still it is not the *opinion* or the *idea* which Jesus had which is significant.

When Jesus washed the feet of his disciples (John 13:5) he further taught the meaning of the yoke. He that serves gives. Follow it.

* * * * *

What special problems does the follower of the Way face today to serve others?

Is the washing of feed commanded by Christ?

How does the future affect your actions? Do you live mainly by the past, present, or future?

How does giving something away keep it for you?

6th Day — Reconcilers

2 Corinthians 5:16-21

A reconciler has many functions. One, he causes people to be friendly again, which assumes of course that enmity had existed. Two, he adjusts or settles differences. People argue over a fence boundary, as an example. Bitter feuds have started over less.

Third, he makes matters consistent; that is, he brings them into line. Fourth, he helps to bring a kind of acceptance among parties of disagreement. Fifth, he may help a person to accept an illness or other affliction.

As can be seen, the function of one who reconciles can involve persons, ideas, or problems. An inconsistency with harmony exists. The reconciler has compassion; he has concern; he wants to make what is crooked straight.

The Christian reconciler does all these things, but he does one very important thing more. Human treaties or agreements are basically selfish documents - *if you do not step on me, I promise not to step on you.*

The one thing *more* the Christian reconciler does is to give divine motivation for reconciliation. The basis for this is Christ's own act of reconciliation, and the Christian belonging to the Way follows Christ's example (2 Cor. 5:18-20). He is a *new creature* (2 Cor. 5:17) if he is in Christ.

Imagine your being *new*, doing things in relationship to people you would not have dreamed possible!

The covenant of Jacob with Laban (Gen. 31) has often been criticized as an expression of distrust. It is impossible to sympathize with this view. To begin, it is the first instance in the Old Testament of a covenant, or agreement, between two human parties. That in itself ought be occasion for rejoicing. They were making history.

Secondly, the name of the Lord was invoked. That counts for a great deal. Third, reconciliation must start somewhere. Even an uneasy agreement is better than none. Build on that to begin. Move further later.

* * * * *

On what basis should Christians settle their own differences?
What is the importance of being reconciled with men? Does it really make any difference if one is reconciled to God? Can the two be separated?

7th Day — Follow Me

John 1:43-51

What is it that forms an opinion? Briefly, it is formed by what a person hears, sees, reads, and what others say. Added to it are his own prejudices, training, education, the nature of his personality, the state of his health even down to his glandular activity.

Some persons have so refined these theories of the forming of opinions they would argue strenuously as follows: "Man is a being controlled so completely by all personal and environmental factors that he is completely predetermined."

That would mean, of course, that particular and special knowledge would enable some people to predict exactly what you and others will do.

Such a person who believes this may be called a determinist or a mechanist. He believes that everybody will follow his pattern; indeed, he is forced to do so and cannot in fact move out of the mechanism which makes up his life.

Imagine having told that to Philip and Nathaniel and the other disciples when Jesus came into their lives and wanted them to follow him (John 1:43)!

Now to be sure, there are opinionated people whose actions can be predicted every time. They are *determined* to be selfish and ignore all reason completely.

There are also people so broad they have no opinions. They are equally *determined* to be liked and will never make up their minds about anything, in order not to offend anyone.

Both kinds of persons have not learned enough yet. The first is inflexible. The other is flabby.

These are common traits and all of us share them to some degree, just as Jacob and Esau shared them. Fortunately, they were able on occasion to be shaken out of the pattern.

This basically is what God does for each of us. He breaks apart in the one case the opinionated and puts iron in the backbone of the other. "Follow me" is a call to a life *determined* by God, not ours but His will.

*   *   *   *   *

Into what category would you put yourself of the two categories described? What other categories are there?

If you believe that there are many categories of persons, are they clearcut or mixtures of all?

The spiritual pilgrimage we take in life when we belong to the Way ought to begin with certain pre-suppositions. *We really do not know very much,* is an important one with which to begin.

All people ought to know that much knowledge is always incomplete in everything they do. No one really knows how to take care of a baby properly but somehow millions of them seem to grow up.

Beyond the thought-forms, the physical handicaps, and the psychological or glandular deterrents which make up individuals, there is a power which lifts us beyond them. It begins with, "Follow me."

ISAIAH 40

8 The grass withers, the flower fades;
   but the word of our God will stand
   for ever.

THE THIRTEENTH WEEK
HE CARETH FOR YOU

Introductory Bible reading for this week:
John 10:7-18

Nothing is clearer in both the Old and the New Testaments than the fact of God's caring for His creation, the world and all people in it.

The theme is repeated in many of the familiar hymns: "Our God our help in ages past, our hope for years to come," "Rock of ages, cleft for me," and "Love Divine, all love excelling," to mention only three.

There are many, however, who say, "This is a child's faith, but for dealing with the hard facts of life, its struggles, and for living as an adult in a hard world, God's caring for us is plainly unrealistic and what is needed are doses in large quantities of human strength."

This is what Christ came to deny by His life and teachings.

1st Day — Protectors of the Flock

John 10:1-6

Family love quite often exhibits both great love and great selfishness. Jealousy frequently also comes into play.

In his old age Jacob believed his son Joesph to have been killed by wild beasts (Gen. 37:33), when in reality his own sons had sold Joseph into slavery. It was Judah who had suggested this rather than have their brother killed, and the exchange was twenty pieces of silver for their brother's life (Gen. 37:26-28).

Later it was Judah who was willing to give himself to Joseph, who had become a ruler in Egypt, though Judah did not know this, in place of Benjamin his younger brother (Gen. 44:33). Judah did this out of the love he had both for his brother Benjamin but especially for his father Israel.

So it is that one begins to understand the motive of Judah. He was not primarily concerned with his welfare but, out of love, he was concerned for the welfare of all the members of his family. Even in the large family, where rivalries can always be intense, he stands as a man who loved the members of his family more than his own life. He was a true protector.

Judah surely faced the hard facts of his day with unusual understanding and sensitivity, perhaps out of the fact that he was from a large family of Jacob but more likely because he had the qualities of heart and mind which meant leadership and even more (Gen. 49:8-12) for the future of his people.

Over all the family scene the God of Abraham, Isaac, and Jacob is the great protector of this family and in a touching blessing Isaac presents this reminder to them all (Gen. 48:15-16).

In later teaching, Jesus likens himself to the protector of the flock, known by those whose shepherd he is.

God cares. Jesus cares. His followers care for others. Both from the Old and the New Testaments once again are reminders of the ways of God.

* * * * *

In the light of the events which occurred later, what would you say was Judah's motive in saving his brother Joseph?

Why do you believe in a large family one member develops traits that are better than others?

2nd Day — Willing To Die

John 10:7-18

A hard-bitten officer in World War II is reported to have said once to his chaplain: "To any one who has met the real things, all your little dogmas about God seem so pedantic and unreal."

The officer no doubt meant by *the real things* the struggle of war, forced marches, men dying, hunger and thirst, weariness, days without sleep and rest, attacks, and men dying for other men.

Even in peacetime one might add to the list people often consider the *real* as contrasted to the *religious* things: the struggle to keep our heads above water, failures in business and marriage, immorality, murders, jealousies, the harm of gossipers, and meaninglessness in daily tasks.

In this contrast, it seems that the real life has it over the religous life. All of the things have been weighed and theologies have come out weakly and found wanting. This life is stronger than God.

There was One who was willing to give his life for others. He said, "I am the good shepherd: the good shepherd giveth his life for the sheep (John 10:11)." God is stronger than this life.

The evidence does not seem all to have been weighed. One could mention the heroisms and victories of war, the triumph of justice in the long run.

Where life is negative men seem to be at fault, not God. Many, by their selfishness, thoughtlessness, ignorance, laziness, lack of discipline, and lack of character create their own failures.

It was Cassius who said to Brutus in Shakespeare's *Julius Caesar:* "Men at some time are masters of their fates: the fault, dear Brutus, is not in our stars, but in ourselves, that we are underlings."

There are too many examples of men and women who have risen above difficult circumstances, ill health, failures, enemies, and countless negative experiences to conclude that victorious living is impossible. Jesus shows the way. God cares.

*　*　*　*　*

What contrasts would you give between the real life and the religious life?

Do you believe that often people do classify Christians as being unrealistic? Why?

Do you know of examples personally where real has been unreal and religious has been untrue?

3rd Day — Abiding In His Love

John 15:1-11

Jesus expects us to share with Him in the responsibilities He has been given by the Father. This means abiding in His word, thus his love (John 15:6, 10).

Though certainly not fully up to New Testament standards, the enfolding of the Genesis story of human searchings reveals an understanding of what was to be revealed fully in Christ. Abel believed in the reality of God, though Cain did not.

Noah trusted God enough to take a step of faith to build the ark. Abraham, Isaac, Jacob and others in their tribe revealed that they understood the reality of God. Perhaps the greatest injustice that could be done to Old Testament thought is to classify it as less significant than New Testament thought because some of the manners of the people were cruder.

Manners of the times, customs we may not understand, have nothing at all to do with the revelation of God or even of man's understanding of them. Men of an earlier age may have had only a partial revelation, but have understood. God did not change. He was always the same.

Abraham had to have understood what it meant to have abided in God's love to have been willing to sacrifice his son, Isaac. Take these thoughts forward to the present.

C. S. Lewis the English writer and Christian, once raised the question, What is theology?

Theology, Lewis believed, is God caring. It is like a map. Merely learning about the Christian doctrines is not exciting. Doctrines are not God. They are only a kind of map, based on the experiences of thousands of people who have really been in touch with God.

That is what *abiding in Him means*. If you want to know what others have known, you must *use* the map. You will not get anywhere by looking at maps if you do not set out to sea. And you will not be very safe if you go to sea without your map and compass.

* * * * *

Respond to the statement that the Old Testament should be rejected because it is a crude representation of the truth about God. Support your answers.

Is your map of theology torn?

What are you doing to mend it?

4th Day — Friends of Christ

John 15:12-17

It is perhaps more significant to say that Judah was a friend to his brothers and his father than to say he was a brother and a son. Brothers and sons have denied their family heritage and have at times brought disgrace on their families.

A friend! He is different. It is perhaps good that Jesus takes in those who love him under the broad and wonderful understanding in the word "friend."

One is not a brother or a son by personal choice. Only a friend falls into the category of an intimate by decision. Jesus certainly gave full scope and significance to the word and all its implications when he said, "Greater love has no man than this, that a man may lay down his life for his friends (John 15:13)," and then He goes further.

His friends are those who do what He commands. He chooses his friends, and then commands his friends to love one another (John 15:14-17).

A vague religion is attractive because it is all passing, all thrills and no responsibility, like watching the waves from the beach and not being on the sea.

One cannot get to New Foundland by studying the Atlantic ocean from a beach resort. One cannot get eternal life either by just *feeling good about God* on picnics, in music, or in smelling flowers without launching out into the unknown to take the voyage.

Suppose you are bitter, are ill, or are troubled in anyway. God equips you with a spiritual nature of unlimited power to transform any kind of suffering into meaning. Jesus is the source of that power.

King Hezekiah said of his sickness: "Lo, it was for my welfare that I had great bitterness (IS. 38:17)," recognizing that even distressing problems can be the *source* of a transformed life.

It was Wordsworth who also gave modern expression to those who are doomed to go in company with sufferings:

In face of these doth exercise a power
Which is our human nature's highest dower;
Controls them and subdues, transmutes, bereaves
Of their bad influence, and their good receives.

* * * * *

"What a friend we have in Jesus," are words of the hymn. What does this thought mean?
How may suffering teach us something about our own friends.
How may suffering teach us something about ourselves?

137

5th Day — Hatred In Return for Love

John 15:18-27

Jesus' teachings here give several examples of aspects of love which are usually misunderstood. Consider them carefully: *hatred by others may be our reward.*

You may reason as follows: "If I do what those in the world desire and treat them decently, then I can expect proper treatment in return from such persons in the world."

What Jesus says is that this *is not true.* If He had not done His works in the world, he would not have been hated (Jn. 15:24) without cause (Jn. 15:25).

It must be admitted that this is unusual thinking compared with the normal understanding of love with which we daily respond to our own loved ones. The basic reason is that *love* in the English language is both a much used and a much misused word. Jesus' teaching must be considered in depth.

When Paul wrote to the Romans, he stated, Let love be genuine (12:9). In effect, Paul is urging Jesus' views. Do not pretend or deceive. Let love be genuine, even when it might be difficult to do God's will.

Joseph was loved by his father, Jacob. Joseph's brothers hated him because of this. It was not the love of Jacob that was wrong. First, he may have shown preference for Joseph in such a way as to make his other sons jealous. Or, there may have been flaws in his sons. Judah was not jealous of Joseph.

Rather, he loved him and showed in many ways his love for all his brothers and his father as well. Judah's love was genuine.

From Genesis to Revelation God's love is the binding thread of Scripture, but do not be surprised if living by God's love produces hate.

Men do not know God. Love them, yes, but as Jesus clearly states, "If the world hates you, know that it has hated me before it hated you (Jn. 15: 18)."

* * * * *

What point basically is involved when Jesus urges love but warns of hatred?
Why do you sometimes hate what you really love?
Why, on the other side, do you sometimes love what you really hate?
What value does love have even when hated?

6th Day — Are You Worthy?

John 16:1-11

The way of *love* is both strange and wonderful! It is strange because it does not follow an expected pattern but God's will demands love. The end result of such *genuine love*, in the long run, is wonderful because it turns the world not upside down but right side up.

The world has never been the same because of God's love through Jesus Christ. Jesus changed values because He changed men's lives.

Jesus' life was one of compassionate ministry to men's needs, to the sick of body, mind, and spirit. He loved the sinner.

Within his own band of twelve men there was bitterness and betrayal and denial, but Jesus over and over again indicated in words and actions His love for them. He loved also those of his enemies who were overly-righteous. He took their jibes, their criticisms of Him and His teachings. He loved all people so much that He could be hard with them when needed as an outgrowth of that love.

If a parent loved a child less, he certainly would allow transgressions go by unnoticed, unmentioned, and unpunished.

Jesus did not live by legalistic rules. He believed in the spirit of the law rather than the law itself, but this does not mean that He ignored the laws of God.

When it is observed how Christian love was practiced by the early Christians, it is quite clear that they followed Jesus' lead. Many people killed Christians and honestly thought they were doing God a service, just as Jesus predicted (John 16:2). They met opposition, but they did not seek to provoke it.

It came because of their belief. They did not set out deliberately to offend, but they did offend.

Jesus' life, teaching, and death exemplified genuine love in action. Had Jesus loved the world less, he would not have challenged the ways of the world.

This is what the Christians of that early day saw and followed. He cared for them. They cared for others.

* * * * *

Why is such a radical love demanded by God?

Can you explain how the sacrifice of your time, talents, and life can produce changes in people?

How does God use us?

What strength ennables Christians to love?

7th Day — The Word of the Center

John 16:16-24

The treatment of *love* this week may have been puzzling for you. There is a reason for this. The virtue of Christ to be magnified above all others is not love. Jesus does not reduce everything to one motive - love.

Jesus nowhere commands love for its own sake. Nowhere does Jesus exhibit the complete dominance of the kindly over the aggressive sentiments. Richard Niebuhr states, "The virtue of love in Jesus' character and demand is the virtue of the love of God and neighbor in God, not the virtue of the love of love." Why?

Niebuhr then goes on to draw a very practical and important conclusion: "Hence the love of God in Jesus' character and teaching is not only compatible with anger but can be a motive to it, as when he sees the Father's house made into a den of thieves or the Father's children outraged."

It was *not love but God* that filled Jesus' soul. "For God so loved the world . . . (John 3:16)," tells the story clearly and simply. Therefore, Jesus enunciates the place of the *first* and *great* commandment (Mt. 22:37-38) *to love God.*

Have you not experienced convincing sweet talk, even apparent kindness and love, only eventually to discover guile and deceit? Of course you have!

Have you not, on the other hand, also experienced the hearing of what seemed to be hard words which eventually proved great love? Ofcourse you have!

Genuine Christian love is not adjustment to the sentiment of love but adjustment to God. With this understanding the present may be sorrowful, but the time will come when you will rejoice (Jn. 16:22).

The center of life an individual sees from day to day is very circumscribed. No wonder it is difficult to grasp so great a love. Christ is the Word of the center of the Christian's life, from which unending love of God pulses out to all the world.

Not all the books of the world could fully explain it (Jn. 21:25).

* * * * *

Is there any place where Jesus teaches us to love love?

Consider the teaching of the prophets. How is their concept of love similar to Jesus'?

What radical adjustment is required of disciples?

Your soul will not develop without going deep into the heart of Jesus' understanding of the will of God.

The power of Jesus in your life, the knowledge of the forgiveness of your sins, and the indwelling of the Holy Ghost are all required to grasp Jesus' teaching about love.

In addition to this inward look, you will also need to look backward over the centuries to the beginnings of man's initial awareness of God. Genesis reveals the goodness of God, His love for all mankind, and it establishes the foundation for His full revelation.

JAMES 4

13 Come now, you who say, "Today or tomorrow we will go into such and such a town and spend a year there and trade and get gain"; 14 whereas you do not know about tomorrow. What is your life? For you are a mist that appears for a little time and then vanishes. 15 Instead you ought to say, "If the Lord wills, we shall live and we shall do this or that."

CONCLUSION

Having established a pattern for daily devotions, you will naturally want to continue.

You should be critical and discerning about your next steps. I would remind you that there are many devotional guides. Some of these are very poor, no more than sentimental gestures in the direction of genuineness. You must make your own examination and judgment. Fortunately, there are many directions you can go, just as there are many varieties of religious experiences and many varieties of ways Christians can come to God.

First, you may seek a book for a guide similar to the pattern you have followed through this book after the first three months of prayer/meditation.

Some of these may be published by your denomination as a "pocket book." Examine it carefully and fairly.

Second, you may wish to read only the Bible for a period of time. The American Bible Society has available annual suggested readings from the Bible which would take you through the Bible in one full year. Or, on your own, you could choose one of the books of the Bible to read, Psalms, one of the prophets, a Gospel, reading not a certain predetermined number of verses, but only as far as you wish to go.

Third, another variation of the above is to add brief readings from one of the devotional classics not related specifically to your daily Bible reading. You will have to keep in mind that the so-called "classics" for the most part were written by monks whose manner of life and aim would present an approach centuries old. It would not be dangerous to separate oneself from the company of others from time to time for prayers, as Jesus did (Lk. 6:12). However, a solitary life should not be permanent.

Fourth, some churches have Bible readings in their hymnals or books of worship, many of which follow the Church Year. Turn to these for a guide.

Fifth, you can ask your pastor for suggestions.

Sixth, you may be inclined to do some library research on your own, using various combinations of approaches.

The possibilities are really quite endless for individual devotions.

Several reminders:

- the elements suggested in this book are important so do not depart too far from them.
- regularity on a daily basis is primary both for Bible reading and prayer.

- acting out your insights daily will insure vitality for your entire life.
- above all, seek God and His will for you, your work, and your life.

No one is going to punish you if you fail to pray and meditate on God's Word daily. You will draw your own conclusions, that you will see great benefits when you persist daily and losses when you do not. You will *want* not to miss. Nothing I write in this regard will be more persuasive than your own positive arguments and conclusions that when you fail to do what you know you ought to do, you only punish yourself.

* * * * * *

The secret place of thunder ... all things burn with the fire of God. To each his own tongue, but He is God.

The sweep of the future is with a renewed Christian Church, not just the Church it now is but the Church it will be. Yet, the Church that will be (names and labels and denominations may give way) will be catholic in its hold of that which is abiding in the Faith once given and protestant in its insistence that the Faith once given is not static but constantly creating and creative — *the Church of the Sign and the Struggle.*

Sign and struggle? Why? *GOD.*

Out of all the secret places of thunder, in our hearts, and in the history of our day, God comes and calls Christians to the task of this and every generation.

He has set us over nations by giving us this place in which to dwell, to pluck up and to break down, to destroy and overthrow, to build and to plant. To see and search out signs. To struggle toward a maturing and sound Christian faith, putting all childish ways firmly aside.

Amen!

DATE DUE